Being Always Peachy

A Year of Devotionals

Published by Safe Haven Farm Press

A.C. Williams
P.O. Box 154
Haven, KS 67543

For more daily devotionals, visit www.AlwaysPeachy.com

All Scripture quotations used in this book are taken from the *Holy Bible*, New Living Translation, copyright © 1996, 2004. Used by permission of Tyndale House Publishers, Inc., Wheaton, Illinois, 60189. All rights reserved.

ISBN-13: 978-0692351246
ISBN: 0692351248

Cover design by Rachel McDonald (http://thegraphicsgirl.com/)

Photography of Entz Orchard in Newton, Kansas, by A.C. Williams

ACKNOWLEDGEMENTS

Being Always Peachy was made possible by generous financial support from:

> Micah Brown
> Marsha Rosson
> Jen Cusick
> Mike and Lisa Phillips
> Dave and Diane Borg

Thank you all for your confidence, your encouragement, and your friendship.

TABLE OF CONTENTS

October – Dealing with Discouragement 217

January 2015

CHANGE

Change is a part of life that no one can escape. No matter how hard you try to avoid it, everything changes. That's why it's so important to build your life's foundation on something that never changes. Because when your life falls apart, the rock you're standing on won't budge.

January 1

God knows how your life will change

IS YOUR LIFE the same today as it was last year? What about last month? Maybe not even a week has passed, and your life has already turned into something you no longer recognize.

Everything changes. Nothing about us or our lives stays the same, and the only way to make it through with your sanity somewhat intact is to hold on to something that doesn't change.

Malachi 3:6
"I am the Lord, and I do not change. That is why you descendants of Jacob are not already destroyed."

God doesn't change. Ever. He's the same now as He was when He created everything. He's the same God who saved Noah and his family, the same God who brought Israel safely out of Egypt, the same God who helped Joseph interpret dreams and David write songs.

The seasons don't shake Him. Our actions don't surprise Him. And even when it feels like everything is spinning out of control, He still knows what He's doing. He hasn't lost control. He hasn't abandoned us. If He didn't abandon Israel, He won't abandon us either. He promised He wouldn't, and He always keeps His promises.

What's the Point?
Whatever you're facing today, just remember that everything about you and around you can turn over on its head, and God will still be the same. You can face change with courage and confident hope because God already has it settled.

You may not know what's coming, but He does. And with His help there's nothing you can't conquer.

January 2

Underdog

UNDERDOG STORIES ARE fun to read. There's something inspiring about an average person who does impossible things, regardless of who they are or what they're trying to accomplish. If it seems impossible, and if the odds are stacked against them, we cheer them on.

And so does God. Did you know that? The Bible is full of underdog stories, where average people like you and me end up in extraordinary circumstances, and through God's power, they change the world.

Zephaniah 3:19
And I will deal severely with all who have oppressed you.
I will save the weak and helpless ones;
I will bring together
those who were chased away.
I will give glory and fame to my former exiles,
wherever they have been mocked and shamed.

The greatest heroes of the Bible have often started out as the lightweights in the corner who didn't stand a chance. But every time they obeyed God, God gave them victory over armies much larger than they were. Average, everyday, unimportant people, some with disabilities or major life challenges, and used them to change the world. Only God can do that.

What's the Point?
Are you facing something impossible? Do you feel unequal to the task in front of you? Guess what? God's cheering for you.

God is a God of underdogs, and He's always looking for people who will answer when He calls. And to those who answer, who are willing to obey, God comes alongside. And with His help, the impossible isn't impossible anymore.

January 5

Tears are okay

LIFE CAN CHANGE drastically without warning, but sometimes it's the changes you know about that can be the most difficult to overcome. You see them coming in the distance, and as much as you try to prepare yourself for them, you still end up in tears at random, inconvenient moments.

So many times, Christ-followers think they have to be dry-eyed and happy all the time, no matter what changes in our lives, but that's not true. Grief is real. But just because you're grieving doesn't mean you'll never feel joy again.

John 16:20
I tell you the truth, you will weep and mourn over what is going to happen to me, but the world will rejoice. You will grieve, but your grief will suddenly turn to wonderful joy.

This is Jesus talking to His disciples, trying to prepare them for His imminent death. But He wants them to be ready for something bigger. He wants them to understand that His death isn't the end. Yes, they were going to grieve when He died, but He wasn't going to stay dead. And after He rose again under His own power, there would be cause for great rejoicing.

What's the Point?
Only God can take something sad and turn it into something worth rejoicing over, and He can do it in the blink of an eye.

Tears aren't wrong. It doesn't make you a bad Christian to be sad. If you follow Christ, whether you're changing jobs or changing friends or changing countries, you can know that God is working things out. You can know it because He told us so.

January 6
Even sunlight fails

HAVE YOU EVER seen an eclipse? They're pretty amazing because we know what they are, but thousands of years ago, I'm sure it must have really freaked people out. After all, sunlight was supposed to be constant and unwavering. Imagine being a sun-worshiper and having your god vanish!

For me, an eclipse exists for one purpose: to demonstrate that even sunlight isn't constant.

James 1:17
Whatever is good and perfect comes down to us from God our Father, who created all the lights in the heavens. He never changes or casts a shifting shadow.

The statement "never changes or casts a shifting shadow" actually references the rising and setting of the sun. The part about a shifting shadow is in reference to an eclipse.

Isn't that cool? The Book of James might have been written as early as A.D. 45, and the fact that we can find something like this in there is awesome!

What's the Point?
Trusting things we can explain is easy. That's why we make up unfounded explanations about things we don't understand. That's what people did with eclipses until science could explain them.

But you can't explain God. Not really. And that's okay because God is good, and He never changes.

Nothing can eclipse God. He doesn't rise or set like a sun. He is constant. And that's great news for us because life is too much for us to handle alone. And it's nice to remember that even if the sunlight fails, God never will.

January 7

A foundation stronger than circumstance

BUILDINGS NEED STRONG foundations if they want to survive storms, but the same is true in your everyday life. If you don't have a solid foundation, the storms of life can rock your world. But they don't have to be giant storms. Even little cracks in a foundation are a big problem. Just like everyday issues can chip away at you until you've become someone you never intended to be.

Psalm 62:6
He alone is my rock and my salvation, my fortress where I will not be shaken.

Even if you have a strong foundation, life is still going to throw curve balls at you. Even if you're firmly grounded, you will still experience earthquakes. Just having a strong foundation doesn't mean change won't affect you. But the strength of your foundation will determine how you handle the experience.

If your foundation isn't strong enough, everything you build on it will suffer. Some foundations wear away with time. Or they erode. Or they just weaken. Maybe they started out strong, but as the years pass, they just wear out because what they're made of isn't a good enough material for building.

What's the Point?
What are you building your life on? Yourself? Your friends? Your job? None of that is good enough.

Build your life on Christ, the Rock that doesn't change. Make decisions based on what the Bible says. Live your life the way Christ did. Then, your foundation will be strong enough to withstand any storm, which means the rest of your life will be too.

January 8

When everything changes, God is good

SURROUNDING YOURSELF WITH good people is a good idea. You can usually trust they'll do what's right, even when it's difficult. Good friends can help you make good decisions.

So if it's wise to have friends who are good, wouldn't it be even better to keep God's instructions close? Because that's one of the amazing things about God. He truly is good.

Deuteronomy 32:4
He is the Rock; his deeds are perfect.
Everything he does is just and fair.
He is a faithful God who does no wrong;
how just and upright he is!

There's no second guessing with God. If He does something, it's good. The Bible says that over and over and over again. But if that's the case, why is the world broken? If God were good, wouldn't He fix it?

I don't claim to understand God. Nobody can. But the Bible says He's good, and that means He is.

The world isn't good. I'm not good. People aren't good. But God is. And He is working to make things good again for the people who follow Him.

What's the Point?
The world is changing by the hour, and many of those changes are bad. But because I know that God is good, I trust that He can take even the ugliest situation and make it beautiful.

So when everything goes wrong today, remember God is good. No, we may not understand what's happening or why, but if you're a Christ-follower, nothing can happen to you that God can't use for good.

January 9

Focus doesn't happen by itself

WHEN LIFE CHANGES without warning, I lose focus really easily. I get stressed out, and then I start doing things that are easy instead of things that are right.

If we're not careful, we'll allow the stress in our lives to dictate how we live instead of obeying God. We need focus to keep God in our sights, but focus doesn't happen by accident.

Romans 12:21
Don't let evil conquer you, but conquer evil by doing good.

No, you didn't read that wrong. At first glance, you might not think this verse has anything to do with learning how to focus, but think again.

It takes a lot of focus (and God's help) to do what's right because our default setting is to do wrong. Our natural state as a sinner is to live in chaos, but God isn't a God of chaos. He's a God of peace and order. And with His help, we can overcome our default settings and climb out of the chaos of an ordinary life.

But you can't just sit back and will your life to change. It takes effort, intention, and God's power.

What's the Point?
Choose now how you'll handle the wrongs you encounter. It takes effort. It takes time. It takes risk. It takes focus.

So focus on what's good and then do it, especially to those who are bound by evil. You never know how God is going to use you and your choices to help someone else.

January 12

When everything changes, God doesn't

DO YOU KNOW people who keep their promises? They're good people to know. But how many times does someone have to keep a promise before it becomes part of their character?

The amazing thing about God (one of the many) is that He has made thousands and thousands of promises, just that we know about in the Bible, and He has kept every single one.

Isaiah 44:8
Do not tremble; do not be afraid.
Did I not proclaim my purposes for you long ago?
You are my witnesses—is there any other God?
No! There is no other Rock—not one!"

God has been keeping promises for thousands and thousands of years. The Bible is proof of what He has done and why He has done it. And since He has been keeping promises for so long, why would He stop now?

God doesn't change. In our whole life, He is the one person that doesn't. Life happens. People die. Babies are born. People get married. People get divorced. People move and leave and return. Churches change. Jobs change. Governments change.

What's the Point?
In our lives on Earth, there's only one constant: Everything changes. Change isn't always bad, but change we can't control scares us. But even when everything around us changes, God doesn't.

No matter how topsy-turvy everything in our lives gets, God is still working things out. He promised He would. And if God has kept His promises for all these thousands of years, He isn't going to stop now.

January 13

Do not be afraid to change your plans

I HAD A PLAN in high school. I would graduate from Pensacola Christian College in four years with a degree in commercial writing, but I wouldn't get a full-time job after graduation because I was probably going to get married and start a family.

I made it a year at Pensacola Christian College. I finished my writing degree at Wichita State University. I've been working full time since 2005, and I still haven't even been on a date.

You could say my plan didn't work.

Proverbs 19:21
You can make many plans, but the Lord's purpose will prevail.

People get attached to their plans and are often scared to change them. But I've learned that God's plans are usually better. I could have forced my plan. No one made me leave Pensacola, and I didn't have to go to WSU. I could be married now. Most of my friends are married. Many of them have kids–more than one kid. Some have armies!

But when I consider all that God has given me because I changed my plans to suit His, I wouldn't go back for anything.

What's the point?
We're afraid of the unknown. Once you sit down and plan something, you have the illusion that you're in control, but you're not. Life always happens, and God is the only one big enough to take the broken pieces and make something beautiful out of them. You aren't big enough to do that.

Don't be afraid to change your plans. Even if your plan is good, His is best.

January 14

Name it and claim it?

DID YOU EVER scribble your name on your lunchbox? Or on a toy you loved? Even as children, we understand that if you write your name on something, that indicates it belongs to you or that you are taking responsibility for it.

But it doesn't stop with identifying our toys. Manufacturers of everything from cars to life vests on board ships put labels on things to indicate they made them.

Isaiah 62:2
The nations will see your righteousness.
World leaders will be blinded by your glory.
And you will be given a new name
by the Lord's own mouth.

Receiving a new name is an exciting prospect, but there's a part of naming that people forget. If you name something, usually that means it belongs to you. And honestly, that's how it works with God. But then, who else would be willing to take responsibility for the out-of-control mess that is my life?

If God has changed your name, He has taken responsibility for you. He has the right to tell you how to live.

What's the point?
So if you are a Christ follower, don't think that you choose your own path without consequences. If you've chosen to follow Christ, God has renamed you, given you a new identity, and given you a new path to walk.

God is a God of second chances and third chances and fourth chances and fifth and so on and so forth. He never gives up on us, and He's always there waiting for the day when we realize we can't handle life on our own.

January 15

Does your shadow ever leave?

I AM ALWAYS amazed at how big God is. If you want to feel small, go outside on a crisp winter night and try to count the stars, and then remember that God knows each one of them by name.

But even though God is bigger than we can possibly imagine, God wants a relationship with us.

Genesis 46:3-4
"I am God, the God of your father," the voice said. "Do not be afraid to go down to Egypt, for there I will make your family into a great nation. I will go with you down to Egypt, and I will bring you back again. You will die in Egypt, but Joseph will be with you to close your eyes."

The Bible is full of stories when God spoke to regular people, all through the Old Testament. But when God spoke to people, it was never as a distant or indifferent figurehead. It was always as a personal, real, relevant Person.

In this instance, God is talking to Jacob, one of the founders of Israel, and assuring him that He wouldn't leave him.

What's the point?
No matter where God takes you, He'll never leave you. You can't run from God. It's like playing hide and seek with your own shadow.

So don't be afraid of making hard choices and stepping away from your comfort zone.

God doesn't live in your comfort zone, and He's waiting for you get out of it and come to where He is.

January 16

God sets your appointments

HAS GOD EVER told you to do something that makes no sense? When He tells you (and it's undoubtedly Him) to give money you don't have, to go somewhere you can't afford, to help someone you don't like, what do you do?

Many times there is an urgency to it. He wants us to do it now. Don't hesitate. Just do it. Just jump in and swim. Have you ever thought about the reason why?

Acts 8:26
As for Philip, an angel of the Lord said to him, "Go south down the desert road that runs from Jerusalem to Gaza."

Philip was one of Christ's original disciples. He had an effective ministry in Samaria, but starting in verse 26, an angel pops up in Philip's path and tells him to leave. It seems kind of strange, but what does Philip do?

He left. And on the way, he met an Ethiopian and led him to Christ. The Ethiopian then went out and spread the gospel further. If Philip hadn't introduced him to Jesus, that never would have happened.

What's the point?
There are no coincidences in life. Monumental events don't just happen; they are designed.

If God has told you to change something in your life, don't wait until tomorrow. Don't wait until you are ready. Just do it.

If you don't, you might be late for the appointment God has already set for you. And while it won't be the end of the story, it might be the end of your opportunity to make a difference.

January 19

Status quo

PEOPLE ARE CREATURES of habit. Most people I know initiate change as a preventative measure, not because they enjoy it.

But change is essential. Without change, we don't grow. Without change, we plateau. Without change, we get comfortable, not only with ourselves but with God.

Genesis 12:1-3
The Lord had said to Abram, "Leave your native country, your relatives, and your father's family, and go to the land that I will show you. I will make you into a great nation. I will bless you and make you famous, and you will be a blessing to others. I will bless those who bless you and curse those who treat you with contempt. All the families on earth will be blessed through you."

This guy, Abram (also called Abraham) made a choice to follow God, and it changed his life and our lives and the lives of everyone else on Earth. God told him to leave his home, his family, his life. Just go. And he did.

Does that mean we have to live a life of constant change? That status quo is bad? Well, not necessarily. But if God has told you to change, you need to do it.

What's the point?
Change is uncomfortable, but it helps me remember that I'm not in control and that I need God's help.

But if God has called you to change something in your life, don't be afraid of it. If He's called you to change, do it. God's already worked out the details. He just needs us to say yes and take that first step, even if we can't see where we're going.

January 20

Clinging to God when everything changes

CHANGE IS A PART of life. People come. People go. They get married. They get divorced or maybe they stay together and move on. Relationships form and end, and even if friendships last an extended time, they don't look the same as they did when they started.

Nothing ever stays the same … except God, of course. That's what's nice about being a Christian. Even if the whole world is spinning out of control, you can cling to God and know that you won't lose your footing.

Ruth 1:14
And again they wept together, and Orpah kissed her mother-in-law good-bye. But Ruth clung tightly to Naomi.

Ruth was a foreigner who chose to live with her Israelite mother-in-law Naomi. If you don't know the story, you should read it. Basically, God takes Ruth from obscurity and raises her up to become a pillar of Jesus' family tree.

But at this point in her story, Ruth has lost everything. In a flash, Ruth went from security to acute loss, and nobody would have blamed her for going back to her own country. But she didn't. She clung to Naomi instead.

What's the point?
When we face change, we can put on the brakes and retreat to comfortable ground, or we can give the accelerator to God and hold on.

Going back may be comfortable, but you might be giving up your part in God's story. It may be easier, but is it worth it?

January 21

Everything changes

IF WE KNOW change is inevitable, why do we get so attached to the way life is today? Is that just the way we are? Change bothers some people more than others, but I think all change is difficult at some level, even if you like change.

I don't. I understand why it's important, but I don't like it. It's bad enough when it's change I initiate.

John 14:27
I am leaving you with a gift—peace of mind and heart. And the peace I give is a gift the world cannot give. So don't be troubled or afraid.

Jesus said this to His disciples shortly before His death, and they liked it about as much as I would have. One of the many things I love about Jesus is that He understands exactly how much we want to control our lives, but He also knows that if we actually had that power, we wouldn't do a very good job of managing it.

If I wanted to control my life and manage my circumstances effectively, I would have to know everything, not just about myself but about the people around me. And I can't do that.

What's the point?
God knows how frustrated we get when we realize just how not-in-control we are, and that's where this verse comes in. Jesus didn't leave the disciples without hope. God hasn't abandoned us. Even when He isn't speaking or moving in a way we can see, that doesn't mean He isn't working.

Because we know that, we can choose to be at peace during times of inevitable change.

January 22

God is faithful through the seasons

SUMMER IS A FUN time of year when you're a little kid, but as a grown-up, summer's just hot. Winter's the same way, magical for children and a hassle for adults.

I think there are seasons in our lives like summer and winter. Long. Uncomfortable. Expensive. But I believe God gives us seasons in our lives just as He gives us seasons on our planet.

Joel 2:23
Rejoice, you people of Jerusalem!
Rejoice in the Lord your God!
For the rain he sends demonstrates his faithfulness.
Once more the autumn rains will come,
as well as the rains of spring.

For me, with every change of the season comes a time to rejoice. Because the one constant in life is that everything changes, except God. Though every part of our lives may turn upside down and all the way around, God remains the same. He is faithful.

No matter what season of life you're in, God is there. If you're in the spring and everything is new and exciting and fresh, He'll walk beside you and show you new things you've never seen before. If you're in the winter and life looks barren, He's right beside you, giving you the strength to make it through the day.

What's the point?
God is faithful. He never leaves us. He never abandons us. And He sends little reminders to help us see Him when we forget to look for Him. Like rain. Like sunshine. Like pumpkin scones.

So rejoice. Today is a new day, and God will show Himself to you if you let Him.

January 23

Change stinks ... or does it?

I AM A CREATURE of habit, so change is hard for me, regardless of what is changing. I've learned, though, that sometimes change is good. And sometimes change is necessary because the way things are could be better.

Hebrews 7:25
Therefore he is able, once and forever, to save those who come to God through him. He lives forever to intercede with God on their behalf.

This verse is talking about Jesus being our High Priest. Through Jesus, we have direct access to God Himself. Because Jesus gave His life as a sacrifice for our sins, we don't have to go to a priest to ask for forgiveness. We can just ask for ourselves. We no longer need anyone to stand between us and God; Jesus already did that once and for all.

What Jesus did on the cross changed everything. Jesus' sacrifice for us was another example of God reaching down to us to save us.

What's the point?
Some things have to change. Some things need to change. And God had been planning this specific change since the beginning of time. For thousands of years, God had been promising that the old system would go away in favor of a New Covenant.

Change is scary. It's unknown and it always presents a risk because you don't know what else changing your life will affect. But if you trust the person who's making that change, there's a really good chance that the results will be better than what you have right now.

January 26

Wardrobe malfunctions

WHEN YOU HAVE changed inside, how do you show it on the outside? If your heart changes–well, you still look the same. That's what's difficult about change; most of the time you have to take people's word that they have.

Until you get to see how someone has changed, you won't really know that the change was real, no matter if they claim it was or not. But God knows.

Joel 2:13
"Don't tear your clothing in your grief,
but tear your hearts instead."
Return to the Lord your God,
for he is merciful and compassionate,
slow to get angry and filled with unfailing love.
He is eager to relent and not punish.

In the culture of the Old Testament, it was common to tear your clothes as a symbol of intense grief, an outward expression of sorrow. In our culture, instead of tearing clothes, we call press conferences to offer tearful apologies or go on talk shows to humbly tell our side of the story. But apologizing isn't about telling the world you're sorry. Apologizing is to recognize you've done wrong, accept responsibility for it before God, and choose not to do it again.

What's the point?
God sees our hearts. Putting on a show for Him doesn't work. He's not interested if it isn't real.

Change your mind, and God will change your heart. He doesn't care how sorry you look. If all you've done is put on a good show, maybe you'll have people fooled, but as far as God is concerned, you'll just have a ripped up shirt.

January 27

God changes people

RULES AREN'T BAD, but if you love them too much, they can become something you use to stop challenging yourself. The trouble with rules is that they usually do go hand-in-hand with a performance-based mentality.

2 Corinthians 3:18
So all of us who have had that veil removed can see and reflect the glory of the Lord. And the Lord—who is the Spirit—makes us more and more like him as we are changed into his glorious image.

Thanks to what Jesus did for us on the cross, God made a New Covenant with us. The New Way, salvation through faith in Christ, means we don't have a rulebook to follow. We just believe, and the longer we follow Jesus, the more His Spirit changes us to be more like Jesus.

Rules are good, but it isn't the rules that saved us. Jesus did that. But even if you believe in Jesus as the only way to be saved, you can still be held captive by the rules. It should be Jesus calling the shots in your life—not rules.

What's the point?
Follow Jesus. Turn toward Christ and pull off the blinding veil of the Law that tells you that you have to perform.

If you're tired of trying to change and always failing, get to know Jesus. He wants to know you. And the more you hang out with Him, the more you'll become like Him. Rules have nothing to do with it.

January 28

Changing the way others see you

WHEN YOU CHANGE, people look at you differently. I've always figured it's because being different makes you stand out, and once you stand out, it's hard to fit in again. When we change to be more like Jesus, people notice.

Genesis 41:45
Then Pharaoh gave Joseph a new Egyptian name, Zaphenath-paneah. He also gave him a wife, whose name was Asenath. She was the daughter of Potiphera, the priest of On. So Joseph took charge of the entire land of Egypt.

If there had ever been a person who deserved a break it was Joseph. Joseph wasn't Egyptian. He was Israelite. This verse comes after Joseph interpreted the Pharaoh's dreams and pretty much saved the nation of Egypt, which would pretty much save the entire region during the years of famine.

If you know the story, you know the first time Pharaoh met Joseph, he was a prisoner, accused of rape. But when Joseph was done, Pharaoh understood something: Joseph knew the true God. Not one of their fake, false Egyptian deities. That made enough of a difference to Pharaoh that he changed his view of who Joseph was, to the point where he changed Joseph's name.

What's the point?
When people look at us, they aren't just seeing us. If we've chosen to follow Christ, we are His ambassadors to a world that doesn't want anything to do with Him.

If someone who doesn't believe is watching your life, what do they see? Do they see a life that's worth changing their own life for?

January 29

How do you know who you are?

PEOPLE IN OUR CULTURE derive their identity from their sexuality or their heritage or from religion or from any number of superficial labels. But our identities need to come from something deeper, otherwise our purpose will be equally as superficial.

Genesis 17:5
What's more, I am changing your name. It will no longer be Abram. Instead, you will be called Abraham, for you will be the father of many nations.

Names identify us. Names indicate hopes and dreams for who we will become. Many times names in the Bible actually do end up representing who a person truly is inside. So it's significant that God changed Abram's identity, so Abraham would change how he saw himself.

If you follow Christ, you should understand that you aren't good enough to get to heaven on your own, but that God thought you were worth sacrificing His Son for. Surrendering your heart to Christ is the first step in figuring out who you were meant to be.

What's the point?
With every step closer to Christ, He continues to change us. We grow a little each day. So if you don't know who you are or if you're tired and frustrated with yourself, follow Christ.

The core of who you are will stay the same. After all, God created you to be who you are for a reason, but your perspective will change. The desires of your heart will change. And that's not something you can do on your own; that's something only God can do.

January 30

Do we have to deserve mercy?

DOES SOMEOME have to deserve mercy for us to offer it? But what's the point of showing mercy to someone who has no intention of using it? Mercy is something that is given to you to use, but we have a choice in how to use it. We can either use it to help other people, or we can choose not to.

Jeremiah 7:5-7
But I will be merciful only if you stop your evil thoughts and deeds and start treating each other with justice; only if you stop exploiting foreigners, orphans, and widows; only if you stop your murdering; and only if you stop harming yourselves by worshiping idols. Then I will let you stay in this land that I gave to your ancestors to keep forever.

God knows my heart, and He knows your heart. God knows whether or not we will take advantage of His mercy. He has every right to withhold it until we come to our senses and live the way He's told us to live. But that's God. He has that prerogative and right, and He is justified.

But I'm not God. I'm nobody. I'm just a little beggar who made a choice.

What's the point?
God showed me mercy when He saved me, so I want to live a merciful life. Maybe someone will take advantage of it, but until you give people a chance, you'll never know.

I didn't deserve mercy when God forgave me. So why should I demand that someone else deserve it when I didn't?

February 2015

ENDURANCE

The Bible compares our lives to a race in many different places, and if you think about it, that's a good comparison. We may not be competing, but we do have a long way to travel, most of it's uphill, and it takes lots of endurance to finish.

Endurance is different than strength. Strength is the ability to bear great weight. Endurance is the ability to keep going, even when you want to give up.

February 2
Running from trouble gets you nowhere

MY HOUSE IS FULL of spiders, and they all love to jump out and scare me. Especially wolf spiders. But I made a decision years ago about how to handle spiders: I squish them. Squealing and running away doesn't make them leave. You have to do something.

But what if I hadn't made that decision? I would run screaming every time I saw a spider. The spiders aren't going to change, but how I respond to them can.

Lamentations 3:30
Let them turn the other cheek to those who strike them
and accept the insults of their enemies.

Everyone has enemies. Maybe not enemies in the normal sense of the word. But we all have people in our path who become obstacles to us achieving our potential, and dealing with those people can be difficult. So we have to decide how we're going to handle those people before we meet them. Sometimes, it's better to be the one who backs off. Sometimes, it's better to be the one who takes it on the jaw.

What's the point?
We all have the same problems. They just look different. And if you run from one, you'll find it again a little farther down the road. So stop running. Face your troubles. Let God make you strong and show you what you need to learn.

Spiders come in every shape and size, but they all squash the same. Don't run. Learn how to deal with the small ones, and the big ones won't bother you.

February 3

Out of sight, out of mind

I'VE GOT TROUBLES. How about you? My life blows up on occasion, and I want God to fix it. But He doesn't always work like that. Actually, He rarely works like that.

So I have to go through difficult situations, where people are angry or where people make foolish choices, and I have to pick up the pieces and start all over again. It's discouraging, because trouble is all I can see.

2 Corinthians 4:18
So we don't look at the troubles we can see now; rather, we fix our gaze on things that cannot be seen. For the things we see now will soon be gone, but the things we cannot see will last forever.

God has a plan. Even when nothing makes sense to us, it's comforting to know that He's got it all handled. The trouble with following Christ in this world is that we can't always see the difference God is making, because He's changing people in a way that will last forever, and that's invisible.

What's the point?
We have to trust that He's doing something, even if we can't see it. Especially if we can't see it. We just have to keep doing what we're doing, and we can't give up.

Starting over again is exhausting, and there's always the fear that what we have built will be torn down again. But let's be honest. Sometimes starting life over again is the best thing that can happen to us.

February 4
Getting out of safe mode

HOW MANY TIMES have you tried to open a program on your computer and discovered that something was wrong with it? When that happens, sometimes you get the option to start a program in safe mode. Starting a program in safe mode means that it still functions but some of its options are disabled, allowing you to get your work done without jeopardizing your content. So it works, only with decreased functionality.

Ever get there in life? You're operating but with limited capability, mostly because of physical, mental, emotional, and spiritual exhaustion. Everybody does. The question is: How do you get out of it? With a computer, you restart. But you can't do that with life, can you?

Lamentations 3:22-23
The faithful love of the Lord never ends! His mercies never cease. Great is his faithfulness; his mercies begin afresh each morning.

It's never too late to restart again, not when it comes to your relationship with God. As long as you're still breathing, you still have hope. God never gives up on us, so where do we get off thinking we can give up on Him?

What's the point?
Be honest with yourself. If you need to restart, don't just identify the need and do nothing. Do something about it. Restart. Get back to basics.

Your day started off terrible? It doesn't have to end that way. God loves you. You're valuable to Him. And He wants to hang out with you today.

February 5

Embrace the tough stuff

LIFE IS HARD. That's a fact. So what keeps you going? What gets you out of bed in the mornings? For me, it's coffee. Strong, dark roast with cream.

I'm only being a little facetious. Coffee only gets me so far. It's my desire to do my best for God that takes me the rest of the way. But if you think life is hard, wait 'til you try to live for God.

Romans 5:3-4
We can rejoice, too, when we run into problems and trials, for we know that they help us develop endurance. And endurance develops strength of character, and character strengthens our confident hope of salvation.

When I think of endurance, I think of musicians. That's probably because my mother is a professional musician, a violist. Musicians don't start out knowing how to play or being able to play for hours on end. They have to practice and train to get to that point. It's hard, frustrating work, but it's worth it because when they're done, they can create beautiful music.

What's the point?
Truly following God takes endurance because it's not easy. But if you can push through the challenges you face as a Christ-follower, doing what's right even if you suffer for it, your faith will be so much stronger on the other side. And the greater your faith, the stronger your hope.

Embrace the tough stuff. Just hang on. God will get you through, and when it's done, nothing will shake your confidence in Him.

February 6

Endure suffering like a soldier

I COME FROM a family with a proud military background, dating back to the Civil War. Some marched or drove tanks in World War II. Some fought in Korea. I'm proud of that, and I'm proud to have many friends who are in every branch of the service.

Being a soldier is no small thing. So when the Bible calls Christ-followers soldiers, how should that affect the way we live?

2 Timothy 2:3
Endure suffering along with me, as a good soldier of Christ Jesus.

Soldiers struggle through hardships when they leave home. They're prepared for those challenges, and they face them bravely. And while they don't rejoice to go through those difficulties, they understand it's for a greater purpose. And if that's the way a soldier sees trouble, that's the way I should see it too.

What's the point?
When you face trouble, it's okay to be scared or lonely, but you should place more value on choosing to overcome those feelings than choosing to wallow in them. A soldier looks past the emotion and does what is necessary. And they understand that they don't always need to understand, especially when they have a commander they can trust.

So face the trouble in your life today like a soldier. Endure, understanding that the war won't last forever, and we'll eventually get to go home for the biggest reunion in the history of time. If you can face trouble with that perspective, it'll change the way you see everything.

February 9

How much can you juggle?

DO YOU JUGGLE? I've never been very good at it, only really managing two or three balls at a time. And nothing exciting. Like fire. Or axes. But that's talking literally. Now, figuratively, I'm a spectacular juggler.

We all juggle our careers, our families, our hobbies, our dreams, our responsibilities, and our unpleasant tasks, and the entire purpose in juggling is to be able to accomplish more at one time. If you can do more, you should. But the more you try to do, the more difficult juggling becomes.

Hebrews 10:36
Patient endurance is what you need now, so that you will continue to do God's will. Then you will receive all that he has promised.

Juggling is a wonderful skill. If you have the talent and ability to do it, you should. And sometimes it's good to develop that talent. But you've got to remember why you're doing it, or you'll lose sight of your goal.

Who made you start juggling in the first place? Did anyone give you all that stuff to juggle at all? Or did you just pick it up?

What's the point?
If you're juggling a lot right now, it's okay to be tired. You're working hard. Finish strong, if you can, and know that God can be trusted to keep all His promises.

But at the same time, take a moment to re-examine what you're juggling and why and for whom. You aren't called to juggle ten balls just to prove you can. You might be called to juggle two for the glory of God.

February 10

Endure when God makes no sense

HAS GOD EVER asked you to do something that makes absolutely no sense? Or maybe He's asked you do something you know for sure isn't going to work. What do you do? I laugh for a while, and then I spend some time groaning and sighing. But then I ultimately get up and do it, because I've learned that God always has a reason.

But to get to the point where we trust Him that much, we may have to do some things that sound rip-roaring crazy.

Judges 6:14
Then the Lord turned to him and said, "Go with the strength you have, and rescue Israel from the Midianites. I am sending you!"

This verse is from the story of Gideon, which everyone should read (Judges 6-8). Gideon was a completely ordinary, almost cowardly guy, who God used to save Israel. Gideon planned to defeat an invading army his own way, but God stopped him—and told him to fight with torches and clay pots instead.

And they won.

Seriously. Read it.

What's the point?
Sometimes God's plans sound nuts. God's ideas go against everything we think makes sense. But that's okay. Because He's God, and He doesn't think the way we do.

And maybe it sounds crazy, but the next time God asks you to do something that doesn't make sense, just do it. See what happens. A crazy idea by itself is just crazy. A crazy idea with God's help can achieve the impossible.

February 11

Enduring when God makes you wait

EVERYBODY KNOWS Christ-followers must endure difficult times, but what about enduring times that aren't difficult? What about the times when it feels like all you do is sit? It's that dreadful, empty waiting period in between difficulty and joy.

To me, endurance usually means you're suffering through some kind of trouble. But can you endure through waiting? Is that even endurance?

Hebrews 6:13-15
For example, there was God's promise to Abraham. Since there was no one greater to swear by, God took an oath in his own name, saying: "I will certainly bless you, and I will multiply your descendants beyond number." Then Abraham waited patiently, and he received what God had promised.

Waiting is a part of following Christ, and fortunately the Bible is full of examples of how we should wait (and what happens when we don't). Abraham had to wait until he was more than 100 years old for God to keep His promise. He didn't wait perfectly. He really screwed a lot of stuff up, but when he finally got it through his head to wait for God, God came through.

What's the point?
God has made each of us a promise, and it's our job to trust and wait for Him to work. He will, but it won't be on your timetable. He'll either drag it out, or He'll light a fire under you. Either way, you'll come out the other side stronger than when you started.

God will make waiting worth it. You just do what you're supposed to do today. You never know. Tomorrow, everything might change.

February 12

Living when you know trouble is coming

HAVE YOU NOTICED that the anticipation of pain and difficulty is sometimes worse than the actual pain and difficulty itself is? I think our imaginations convince us it's going to be unbearable, when it really isn't.

But how do you get through? Many times, we know trouble is coming. Things may be quiet now, but trouble is just over the horizon, and we have no choice but to walk toward it and tackle it as it comes. But even if we make that choice, how do you live in the interim?

Mark 10:33-34
"Listen," he said, "we're going up to Jerusalem, where the Son of Man will be betrayed to the leading priests and the teachers of religious law. They will sentence him to die and hand him over to the Romans. They will mock him, spit on him, flog him with a whip, and kill him, but after three days he will rise again."

This is Jesus speaking, telling His disciples what's going to happen to Him before it happens. Can you imagine living life knowing you were born to die a horrible death? Jesus knew, but did His life show bitterness or hopelessness, knowing He was destined to die brutally?

No.

What's the point?
You can anticipate trouble, but you don't have to dread it. Jesus knew what was coming, and He didn't face it with resignation or defeat. He faced it with hope, because He knew God's plan.

And thanks to Him, you can do the same.

February 13

Endure when it feels like nothing changes

WHEN I DO something, I want immediate results. That's why I'm not good at gardening or playing a musical instrument, because I want results right away. I want immediate ROI—return on investment, as we call it in marketing. But I've learned that following Christ is less like marketing and more like farming—it's mostly waiting and praying that your crop doesn't get blown to bits.

Galatians 6:9
So let's not get tired of doing what is good. At just the right time we will reap a harvest of blessing if we don't give up.

Doing good is hard. Christ-followers are called to live by the Bible, and, in case you didn't know, the Bible's not exactly popular anymore. You try to live by the Word, and you get punished. You get called names. People hate you when you've done nothing but love them. And sometimes it's really hard to believe that it's worth it.

But that's where endurance comes in, because things that grow can't be rushed. If you give up too soon, you'll miss out.

What's the point?
God is always working, both in your life and through your life, but it's usually gradual. It's often very slow going. But if you hold on and don't give up and pay attention, you'll see it. Like wheat sprouting from the dirt, bits of green will start to show where there were none before. It's like that with life too.

You'll make it to harvest. You just can't give up.

February 16

Your spirit is stronger than your body

PHYSICAL ENDURANCE DOESN'T just happen. If you're going to run a marathon, you can't just jump up and do it. You have to train to achieve it. It's the same way with spiritual endurance. You can't tackle huge spiritual battles before you've learned how to trust God.

It's easy to train the body, but you won't gain spiritual strength because you have physical muscles. So don't expect to be able to stand against spiritual attacks just because you can benchpress a Volkswagen.

Judges 16:4
Some time later Samson fell in love with a woman named Delilah, who lived in the valley of Sorek.

Samson was a real-life superhero. His tremendous strength came from God, and he was a Judge of Israel (Judges 13-16) before they had a king. But even though Samson had an extraordinary amount of physical power and endurance, he lacked emotional and spiritual strength.

I'm just going to say it: Samson was pretty much an idiot. Read his story. You'll see. And while his physical strength was impressive, his choices weren't.

What's the point?
The world says your body matters most because we can see it, but God doesn't see us that way. Being physically healthy is important, but your physical strength will only last as long as your body does. Spiritual strength will last as long as you do–an eternity. So which one is more important?

Don't let culture dictate what matters most. Yes, be healthy but not at the expense of your soul.

February 17

Obey without understanding

WHEN WAS THE LAST time God asked you to do something that didn't make any sense? He has asked me to take random international trips, to give financially when I didn't have finances to give, to talk to people about things I didn't want to talk about.

And I've done all that, but it makes people look at me really funny, especially when I admit I don't really understand why I'm doing it. Because why would you do something if you don't understand it?

Genesis 6:14, 22
"Build a large boat from cypress wood and waterproof it with tar, inside and out.... So Noah did everything exactly as God had commanded him.

Building a boat doesn't sound crazy to us, but back in the times that Noah lived in, it didn't rain. Not like we know it today. They'd never seen a flood. So all Noah's neighbors had to think he was flipping insane, because there was no way Noah could hide that ark. But God told him to do it. So He did it.

It made no sense to any of them, until the rain started.

What's the point?
Following Jesus means sometimes you have to obey without understanding, and it sounds crazy at first. Then, the pieces of God's plan start snapping into place, and you realize it wasn't crazy at all.

So if you know God is telling you to do something, don't worry about what people say. People always talk. You just do what God says. Whether it's writing a book or quitting your job or filling a giant boat with giraffes, if He's in charge, He'll work out the details.

February 18

Being honest with God

RESPONSIBILITY IS EXHAUSTING, don't you think? I don't even really have that much, but what I do have wears me out. And all I want to do is just give up, leave the dishes to rot in the sink, and go watch a Jane Austen movie. But most of the time, I power through it, and though I finish my duties, my attitude takes a major hit.

Deuteronomy 34:10-11
There has never been another prophet in Israel like Moses, whom the Lord knew face to face. The Lord sent him to perform all the miraculous signs and wonders in the land of Egypt against Pharaoh, and all his servants, and his entire land.

Moses was a hard core kind of a guy. God used him to lead the nation of Israel out of Egyptian captivity, which sounds impressive enough without knowing he was responsible for millions and millions of people. Moses didn't consider himself a leader. He tried to get out of it a couple of times, but God never let him.

What I love about Moses, aside from the fact that he never gave up, is that he was never fake with God. Moses told God exactly what he was afraid of, and God was there to help him.

What's the point?
God is greater than any responsibility you face. Be honest with Him. He knows your heart, He knows what you're scared of, but when you open up and tell Him, it's like letting go. And He can't help you carry anything until you let go of it.

February 19

Enduring when God is silent

I LIKE INSTRUCTIONS. I don't always read them, but it's comforting to know they're there. But anyone who's assembled a piece of furniture knows that sometimes the instructions just don't make sense. What do you do then?

We run into similar roadblocks in life, when we encounter problems and ask God for guidance. And He doesn't answer. What do you do when God stops talking?

Job 13:15
God might kill me, but I have no other hope.
I am going to argue my case with him.

Job lost everything he cared about in a single day because our enemy, Satan, wanted to make a point. Satan wanted to prove that nobody worships God because they want to, and Job proved him wrong. But Job had to suffer through a lot of really horrible things to get to that point. He hadn't done anything wrong, and I'm not sure he ever found out why God allowed such horrible things to happen.

What mattered is that Job didn't turn away from God, even though he feared God had turned away from him.

What's the point?
We all experience situations that seem unfair. It's okay to question. It's okay to talk to God, to tell Him how you're feeling, but remember who you're talking to. God has told us who He is, and if we believe that, we know He never abandons us.

So when God is silent, don't immediately accuse Him of leaving. Instead, be quiet. He might be speaking, and you're just too noisy to hear Him.

February 20

Enduring metaphorical lions

GOD ALWAYS HONORS people who do what the Bible says, but it doesn't always feel like it right away. Actually, at first, it may feel like you're being punished, but there's never been a time when God hasn't provided for his people or protected them when they needed it.

Daniel 6:10
But when Daniel learned that the law had been signed, he went home and knelt down as usual in his upstairs room, with its windows open toward Jerusalem. He prayed three times a day, just as he had always done, giving thanks to his God.

Daniel was a God-follower in a culture that worshiped idols, but he didn't let that stop him from praying--a lot. Then, one day, the king signed a law that stated people had to pray to him.

Now, if this had happened in today's world, a great cry would have gone up on social media. People would have marched in the streets. But Daniel didn't get angry. When the king signed the law, Daniel went home and did exactly what he'd already been doing.

What's the point?
The world is going to make laws that contradict God's Word, and we need to be ready to stand for what God says is right. But that doesn't mean we have to change tactics, if we're already living the way God says is right. You don't have to make a spectacle of yourself to make a difference.

Maybe the lions you'll face are metaphorical, but God can shut the mouths of metaphorical lions just as easily as real ones.

February 23

Enduring when God is hidden

I STAYED AT A Kansas City hotel with a valet service once, and they required you leave your keys with the valet guy while you checked into your room. I did, but I had to come back out for my reservation paperwork. I couldn't find the valet guy with my keys anywhere, and I stood by the side of the car, getting angrier and angrier. I had to check in, but I couldn't check in without my papers.

Then I realized the car was already unlocked. The valet had been watching the whole time and opened the car when I was ready. I just couldn't see him.

Genesis 50:20-21
But Joseph replied, "Don't be afraid of me. Am I God, that I can punish you? You intended to harm me, but God intended it all for good. He brought me to this position so I could save the lives of many people."

Joseph is one of my heroes because no matter how bad his life circumstances got, he never gave up. He went through every horrible thing, but he always believed God could bring good out of it. And in the end, he understood exactly why God had put him through the difficult times.

What's the point?
You can't really see God, but that doesn't mean He can't see you.

If you're going through hard times, just keep going. It may not get better. It might actually get worse. You can trust that God's on the sidelines, helping you when you need it, whether you see Him or not.

February 24

Life may not be as bad as you think

WHAT'S SOMETHING IN your life that is really difficult to endure? Got it? Now, find someone you know and ask them the same question.

If you're honest, I'll bet that person's issues are worse than yours.

1 Thessalonians 5:18
Be thankful in all circumstances, for this is God's will for you who belong to Christ Jesus.

Everyone knows we're supposed to be thankful, and most of the time, we do a pretty good job. But it's very difficult to be grateful when you're doing your best to keep your head above water and more keeps pouring in on you.

But godly gratitude isn't about being thankful when you feel like it or when everything is going right.

What's the point?

When we're struggling and we feel persecuted, it's easy to slip into endurance mode. And endurance is necessary. We need to keep moving forward, no matter what is happening. But we also need to be thankful. And we need to keep our ears open and our eyes off ourselves.

We must endure, yes, but we also must be thankful. Gratitude is perspective. We get so wrapped up in our own stories that it's difficult to remember sometimes that other people might have it worse than we do.

So eyes off yourself. Start listening to others, and you might realize you may not be as bad off as you think you are.

February 25

Walking buddies

SOME TIME BACK, I got to walk along Hadrian's Wall, the ancient Roman fortification in Northern England. The countryside is barren, beautiful, and outrageously steep in places. And I'm not the most graceful or coordinated human being in the world. But I was walking with three trustworthy friends, a guide, my best friend, and my brother. Without them, I would have stayed at the house.

Isaiah 41:10
Don't be afraid, for I am with you.
Don't be discouraged, for I am your God.
I will strengthen you and help you.
I will hold you up with my victorious right hand.

Sometimes life is like walking Hadrian's Wall. You have to watch your feet instead of the scenery because you can't trust your next step.

Life has ups and downs, harsh inclines and steep drops, damp stone steps and uncertain footing, and it can be tempting to give up and stand still. That's why it's important to have a walking buddy who will catch you when you fall.

What's the point?
Everyone is facing something today. Financial challenges. Work challenges. Health challenges. Family challenges. There's a challenge for every person–sometimes more than one, usually more than two or three. But as Christ followers, we're not facing those challenges alone. We just have to remember that.

God has told us not to be afraid and not to be discouraged. He will give us the strength we need to keep moving forward. He is always victorious, and He's offering that help to us today. We just have to take it.

February 26

The basset hound who climbs mountains

I MET BOOKER the basset hound on a mountain hike in Colorado. Sure, he looked awkward and silly, teetering like an overweight slinky up the worn wooden steps, but he was having the time of his life. And when his family started to take him back down the trail, he pushed forward and dragged them to the top.

Have you ever been in that situation? Where you wanted to do more, be more, see more, achieve greater things than you are physically capable of?

Galatians 6:9
So let's not get tired of doing what is good. At just the right time we will reap a harvest of blessing if we don't give up.

Life is difficult, and if you're a Christ-follower, it's worse. Doing the right thing is hard, and at times, you'll want to give up. But if you do, you'll always be tormented by the "what if" questions. You'll always wish you would have stayed the course.

What's the point?

When you dream big, you face big obstacles. Even if you don't dream big, you'll still face challenges in life that are too big for you to tackle on your own. And in those moments, you'll be tempted to just stop trying. But if God has given you a dream, He'll help you see it through.

The thing about God-given dreams is they have to happen when God is ready for them to happen. Life is hard, but don't give up because the view is worth the climb.

February 27

Nobody accidentally finishes a marathon

RACING TOOK AN early hold in my young brain because my dad was a race car driver before he became a professional business type. My earliest memories are sitting in the front seat of his old VW Rabbit pulling the knobs off the dashboard.

Whether you're talking about racing cars or racing people, racing is a sport that requires outrageous endurance.

Romans 12:1
Therefore, since we are surrounded by such a huge crowd of witnesses to the life of faith, let us strip off every weight that slows us down, especially the sin that so easily trips us up. And let us run with endurance the race God has set before us.

Paul isn't talking about racing cars here, of course, but he isn't talking about the 50-yard dash, either. This is a marathon. This is Talladega or the Indianapolis 500. It's not about speed; it's about endurance. And we're not competing against each other to win. Christ has already won the race. He just wants us to finish running it.

What's the point?
Running a marathon is about your choices. You won't finish a marathon by accident. It's a choice you have to make before and during the race, to keep running when you want to quit.

Faith isn't easy. It's not supposed to be. Faith is believing that God's way is better, and that no matter what obstacles are in your way, you'll keep running your race for Him. The goal of this race isn't to win. It's to finish.

March 2015

PRAYER

People turn prayer into a flowery, showy affair, when really all it needs to be is a conversation between you and God. We don't need to use special words or phrases. There are no magic words or rituals. Just tell God what's on your heart and listen to what He has to say.

March 2

What God can do with my story

DO YOU EVER tell God that you're thankful for what He's done in your life? I mean, really. Do you just sit and give Him the credit for everything you have? If you do, that's awesome. We should all do more of that.

But what about taking it a step further? When was the last time you told somebody about something God did for you?

1 Chronicles 16:29-30.
Give to the Lord the glory he deserves!
Bring your offering and come into his presence.
Worship the Lord in all his holy splendor.
Let all the earth tremble before him.
The world stands firm and cannot be shaken.

We need to talk about what God has done. We need to shout it out at the top of our lungs because we're thankful and so that we don't forget. It's one thing to thank God for what He's done in our lives, but it's something else entirely to give Him the credit for our success in front of people who don't believe.

What's the point?

You have a story. God has done something in your life that He hasn't done for anyone else, but who have you told? Do you know people who need to be encouraged? Do you know people who need to know our great God?

God blesses us because He loves us and He promises to take care of us, yes, but He also blesses us so that we can bless others. So don't keep your story to yourself. That's not why you have it.

March 3

Have a conversation with God

HOW DO YOU pray? Do you repeat memorized text or do you read out of a book? Do you use flowery language when you pray or do you pray the way you normally talk? Do you only pray at church or do you pray over your meals or in your morning devotional time, or at some other specified time?

Prayer is one of those things that Christians talk about a lot, but I'm not sure we see it the way God intended.

Matthew 6:7-8
"When you pray, don't babble on and on as people of other religions do. They think their prayers are answered merely by repeating their words again and again. Don't be like them, for your Father knows exactly what you need even before you ask him!"

Prayer isn't some mystical, ethereal, fuzzy, emotional experience of faith. Prayer is talking to God. Just talking. You can recite verses if you want. That's a fine tradition, but do you talk to your friends in verse? When you speak to your family, do you use words written by someone else 100 years ago?

No. If you want your relationship to last, you just talk. You don't use someone else's words; you use your words. Otherwise, it's not you.

What's the point?
There's nothing wrong with liturgy or cute little poems. Those are great traditions. But don't let your traditions become more important than your relationship with God.

If all you pray comes from someone else's heart, you've missed the point.

March 4

Remember who you are talking to

WHEN YOU PRAY, do you start off by telling God how awesome He is? You should. Those are the instructions Jesus gave us.

Did you know the Lord's Prayer is actually a format for how to pray? Not that we have to follow it word for word. God hears our prayers no matter what, but if you want to keep your perspective straight, this helps.

Matthew 6:9
Pray like this:
Our Father in heaven,
may your name be kept holy.

How many times do we demand things from God? I mean, God wants us to ask for things. God wants a personal relationship with us but not at the expense of us forgetting Who He is.

By first acknowledging that He is God and you aren't, it's easier to remember that He knows what He's doing. And it's good to remember what He's already done for you so you'll remember that He's never left you hanging.

What's the point?
Before you jump into your list of requests, start your prayer off by telling God how great He is. Thank Him for specific things in your life. Thank Him for specific events in your life, good or bad. Thank Him for always being there. Actually, once you recognize everything He's done, it's hard to stop thanking Him.

Don't just start demanding things. Once you get in that habit, you begin to think you deserve them. Remember you're talking to the Creator of everything. You have a free pass to His great throne. Don't take it for granted.

March 5

Lose the entitlement mentality

WHEN YOU ASK God for things, do you set your heart on getting them? He's God, after all. God is good, and what I want is good. So surely He'll give me what I want. That's how it works, right?

Matthew 6:10
May your Kingdom come soon.
May your will be done on earth,
as it is in heaven.

Jesus gave us the Lord's Prayer to teach us how to pray, and this is the second step. The first is remembering who God is. The second is learning to care more about life in Heaven than we do about life on Earth. And part of life in Heaven is understanding that God's will is done.

That's obvious, right? But how often is God's will done on Earth? Yeah, not often at all. So if we're praying for God's will to be done here, that means we're willing to give up what we want in favor of what He says is better.

What's the point?
We think God owes us one. No, we'd never say it out loud, but that's how we treat Him. Just remember that God knows your heart.

Just understand that even if you ask for something with the purest motivation, you still may not get it. But that's not because God is being cruel or unkind or just wants to keep you from having fun. It's probably just not time yet. So give it ten years, and then you'll be able to look back and see exactly why He didn't let you have your way.

March 6

If it matters to you, it matters to God

DO PRAYER REQUESTS ever make you roll your eyes? Someone asks for prayer concerning an issue that you think is just silly? Or not worth praying about? Come on, Christian, unscrew the halo for a little bit and be honest. I think every Christian has wondered at the validity of some prayer requests, but that isn't our job.

On that same note, have you ever not prayed about something because you think it's too small to matter?

Matthew 6:11
Give us today the food we need.

Well, it's not shortest verse in the Bible, but it's close. But what does it mean? Are we only supposed to pray for things that we need? What about things that we want? Can't we ask God for those things too? What about our dreams? What about the impossible? Don't we need more than food?

Remember, the Lord's Prayer is an instruction manual. It's like an outline for how to talk to God, and I think Jesus used the daily bread concept to show us that nothing is too small or insignificant to ask God about.

What's the point?
If our example is to pray for bread, we can pray for help finding our keys or that the gallon of gas left in the tank gets us to the next station.

Yes, ask Him for spectacular things, but don't get so focused on those huge flashy things that you forget that sometimes the small things mean the most.

Nothing is too little. If it matters to you, it matters to God.

March 9

Asking forgiveness is for you, not God

I STRUGGLE WITH living in denial sometimes. I can convince myself that just about anything isn't a problem, or at least that anything can be dealt with later. In some cases, this is a big blessing because otherwise I would drive myself crazy with all the things that I can't accomplish.

But what about the stuff that I can fix? That stuff isn't so good to live in denial about.

Matthew 6:12
And forgive us our sins,
as we have forgiven those who sin against us.

Why is it so hard to ask forgiveness? Well, who likes to admit when they're wrong? When I sin on purpose, I get defensive because I know better, and there's some part of me that tells me to sweep it under the rug and ignore it. It's forgiven. It's not a big deal. God knows I'm not perfect.

But if we ignore our sins, no matter how small, we get desensitized and, before long, they become a habit.

What's the point?
Asking for God's forgiveness is more for our benefit than God's because it makes us realize that we need Him and it helps us see that we don't deserve His grace.

Don't ignore your sin to the point that it becomes a habit in your life. Tell God about it. Ask Him to forgive you, and He will. He never refuses to forgive someone who has truly turned from their sin.

March 10

The elephant in the room

HAVE YOU EVER noticed how difficult it is to have a conversation with someone who hasn't done something they know they need to do? Sure, you can talk around the problem, but it's like a cloud that hangs over both your heads, that has a negative effect on your conversation and your relationship. It's like trying to talk to someone who has something in their teeth. Can you focus on what they're saying?

I've noticed that's true in my human relationships. So why wouldn't it be true in our relationships with God?

Matthew 6:12
And forgive us our sins,
as we have forgiven those who sin against us.

If you're holding something over someone else's head, that's what you're focusing on. That's a part of yourself that's tied down. A part of your heart is distracted. And God wants our whole heart. All the pieces not just the ones we're willing to give Him, not the pieces that are perfect or in good order. He wants all of us.

What's the point?
It's important to ask forgiveness for yourself, yes. We all do wrong. We all sin. And we need to acknowledge those sins when we talk to God, but we also need to forgive others who have sinned against us. If we don't, holding that against them will change us, and it will have a negative effect on our prayer lives.

Whatever you're holding on to today, whatever is keeping that elephant in the room, consider letting it go.

March 11

The devil made me do it

IF YOU'RE HUMAN and you're breathing, Satan is going to throw temptation at you to get you to take a wrong step, to get you to compromise your faith, to get you to lose your testimony. That old phrase, "the devil made me do it" doesn't really play. Maybe he suggested it, but if you're a Christ-follower, you have the power to say no. That makes sin your choice.

So it makes sense that God would expect us to pray and ask for help in facing temptation.

Matthew 6:13
And don't let us yield to temptation,
but rescue us from the evil one.

Many times I think I fall into temptation because I don't anticipate it. It sneaks up on me, and I give in because I wasn't ready to defend myself. That's the trick with our enemy. He knows us better than we know ourselves, and he knows exactly what to throw at us to get us to cave. And if we don't expect it, it's easier to give in.

What's the point?
God has given us the power to resist temptation. That's one of the reasons why we have the Holy Spirit, and it's another reason why we have each other to help us stay accountable. I'm not saying we should see Satan under every rock and shrub, but be aware.

Don't be naive. You're going to experience temptation. That doesn't make you a bad Christian. It makes you human. But if you don't want to be a fool, anticipate it. Understand that it's coming. Learn to recognize the tools Satan uses to throw you off track, and ask God to help. He will.

March 12

He answers at the right time

I DON'T LIKE waiting. I want what I want, and I want it now. But the truth is if God gave me my way, I wouldn't be ready. God knows how much I can handle. He knows what I can take. There's a reason why He's withholding the things I want, and it's not to hurt me or cause me pain.

John 14:13-14
You can ask for anything in my name, and I will do it, so that the Son can bring glory to the Father. Yes, ask me for anything in my name, and I will do it!

That's quite a promise. And if you've ever put it to the test, I'm sure you've experienced the same frustration I have. God works on His own timetable. And it's in those moments that I forget who He is and treat Him like a genie in a lamp, my personal wish granter. And that's not God.

What's the point?
Waiting stinks, but there's always a reason for it. Maybe you need to grow. Maybe someone else needs to grow. Maybe circumstances or seasons need to change. Whatever it is, God knows, and He's not going to interrupt His great plan to grant us our good request.

He's not ignoring you. He's not trying to hurt you. He's not testing your patience. He's waiting for the right time to give you more than what you asked for.

He won't answer when you want Him to. He'll answer when it's time.

March 13

Afraid to pray out loud

PRAYERS DON'T HAVE to be complicated. I'm not sure where the concept of ritualistic prayers came from, but they're not necessary if you want to talk to God. You don't have to speak a different language to talk to Him. You don't have to wax long and eloquent with phrases that sound impressive. If you're going to pray, just talk to Him.

1 Kings 18:36-37
At the usual time for offering the evening sacrifice, Elijah the prophet walked up to the altar and prayed, "O Lord, God of Abraham, Isaac, and Jacob, prove today that you are God in Israel and that I am your servant. Prove that I have done all this at your command. O Lord, answer me! Answer me so these people will know that you, O Lord, are God and that you have brought them back to yourself."

This is a prayer that the prophet Elijah prayed at a really crucial time in Israel's history. If you want the full version, check out 1 Kings 18 on your own.

There's not much to that prayer, but God answered it. In a big way.

What's the point?
We make such a big deal out of prayer. Yes, prayer is a big deal, but we don't need to flail around and make a big show when we're talking to God. He doesn't need that. He doesn't need fancy words or impressive vocabulary. Now, if you pray that way normally–if that's the way you talk–that's one thing. But if you're putting on a show when you're talking to God, it's not for Him.

March 16

How do you pray and believe?

WOULDN'T IT BE nice to know that you would get everything you prayed for? But prayer doesn't work like that, does it?

Have you ever been in that situation where God didn't answer your prayer? You were angry. You were heartbroken. But years down the road, you were able to look back and understand.

Mark 11:22-24
Then Jesus said to the disciples, "Have faith in God. I tell you the truth, you can say to this mountain, 'May you be lifted up and thrown into the sea,' and it will happen. But you must really believe it will happen and have no doubt in your heart. I tell you, you can pray for anything, and if you believe that you've received it, it will be yours."

This passage used to confuse me. I could whole-heartedly believe that God would answer my prayers, but there just seemed to be prayers God would ignore. I didn't understand it, and I thought that maybe God's silence was due to my lack of faith.

But now I've lived a little more, and I've gotten to know God better. And I don't think that's the case at all. It's not necessarily because we lack faith, and it's definitely not because God isn't listening. It's because we expect God to answer us the way we want.

What's the point?
God will answer our prayers, but He'll do it in His own way. Ask Him for what you want, but believe that God is going to do what He wants before He does what you want. Why? Because He knows better.

It's not that He's not answering our prayers. He is. He's just not doing it the way we want. And in the grand scheme of life, which would you prefer?

March 17

Still, small voice

WHEN YOU'RE HAVING a conversation, is there anything more important than talking? What about listening? You can't have a real conversation if both people aren't listening.

So what makes us think that prayer is different?

1 Kings 19:11-13
"Go out and stand before me on the mountain," the Lord told him. And as Elijah stood there, the Lord passed by, and a mighty windstorm hit the mountain. It was such a terrible blast that the rocks were torn loose, but the Lord was not in the wind. After the wind there was an earthquake, but the Lord was not in the earthquake. And after the earthquake there was a fire, but the Lord was not in the fire. And after the fire there was the sound of a gentle whisper. When Elijah heard it, he wrapped his face in his cloak and went out and stood at the entrance of the cave. And a voice said, "What are you doing here, Elijah?"

It's so easy to be busy and loud and frantic, but if we're so busy running around, how do we expect to hear what God wants to tell us? If we're too busy to read scripture, how can we expect Him to communicate with us? I mean, yes, God finds ways to communicate with us, but His primary means of speaking is through the Bible.

What's the point?
God speaks every moment of every day, mostly through the Bible, sometimes through nature, other times through the Spirit. But He never stops speaking.

Are you being still enough to hear?

March 18

Praying for flash drives and itch cream

I LOVE TO TRAVEL, but hauling luggage around is a pain. So I pack light. And usually finding my stuff isn't a problem, but whenever you travel with other people, you always run the risk of misplacing your things in their things. One particular trip, I managed to misplace a tube of anti-itching cream, which was certainly replaceable, and my flash drive, which was not.

I turned our hotel room upside down. I was struggling with a bad rash on my back, and the itching cream helped. But I was more concerned about the flash drive, because it holds the last 20 plus years of my creative life on it.

When I was at the end of my rope, I prayed. And, yes, I found them both, which made me wish that I had prayed about it sooner. But who prays for itching cream and flash drives?

Ephesians 6:18
Pray in the Spirit at all times and on every occasion. Stay alert and be persistent in your prayers for all believers everywhere.

Do you ever not ask Him for something because you're afraid He'll think you're being silly? Well, stop that train of thought right now because the Bible says to pray about everything, all the time, everywhere.

What's the point?
No request is too small for God, whether it's something big like a flash drive that stores 20 years of creativity or a tube of anti-itching cream that only halfway works.

Don't let the world dictate what God will do for you and what He won't.

March 19

God does great things for grateful people

HOW DO YOU react when God answers your prayers? I mean, we're supposed to expect that God will do great things, but what do you do when He actually does? How do you respond? It's at those times that I really don't know what to do or say.

Luke 17:11-16
As Jesus continued on toward Jerusalem, he reached the border between Galilee and Samaria. As he entered a village there, ten lepers stood at a distance, crying out, "Jesus, Master, have mercy on us!" He looked at them and said, "Go show yourselves to the priests." And as they went, they were cleansed of their leprosy. One of them, when he saw that he was healed, came back to Jesus, shouting, "Praise God!"

I try not to get my hopes up when I ask God for big things. I believe that He will answer and give me what I'm asking for in His time and in His way, but I usually expect that time to be later and that way to look completely different than what I expect. But every now and then He gives me exactly what I ask for exactly when I ask for it.

It's then that I need to remember to thank Him. That's the response I need to have because the Bible is clear that God does great things for grateful people.

What's the point?
Take a minute and think about the last prayer God answered for you. Have you thanked Him?

Don't be like the nine men who went away healed and forgot to acknowledge Who was responsible. Be like the one who came back.

March 20

Peace like a security system

REAL PEACE IS elusive in our world, whether you're talking about the peace between nations or people or peace of mind. People pay extravagant sums of money for peace of mind, so they don't have to worry. But is real peace something you can buy? Or is it something you're given?

Philippians 4:6-7
Don't worry about anything; instead, pray about everything. Tell God what you need, and thank him for all he has done. Then you will experience God's peace, which exceeds anything we can understand. His peace will guard your hearts and minds as you live in Christ Jesus.

Have you ever experienced peace that guards your heart? To a natural worrier like me, that sounds awfully nice. I have a vivid imagination, and I can just see worries creeping around in my heart and mind like thieves or robbers. And peace, like a guard or a soldier, beats them back and tells them to hit the road.

Worry is like having a guard available and choosing to guard the door yourself anyway. It's like having a security system installed and sitting up all night in spite of it because you're sure it's not going to work.

What's the point?
Everyone worries, but if you're a follower of Christ, you can pray about it instead of worrying, and God has promised to send His peace–peace so awesome we don't understand it, peace strong enough to protect our heart and our mind from worry. But that protection won't do us any good if we refuse to be protected.

March 23

Fearing trouble

TROUBLES COME. That's just life. But when trouble after trouble after trouble comes pounding at the door, I get tired.

Yes, each trouble is interspersed with great and joyful things, happy things, wonderful things, but it's like the roller coaster of life never really ends, and I can't help but feel like the ride is just starting. For every exciting hill we crest and coast down at top speed, there's another mountain to climb. And climbing up is always harder than coasting down.

But that doesn't mean we have to fear trouble.

Psalm 46:1-3, 10-11
God is our refuge and strength,
always ready to help in times of trouble.
So we will not fear when earthquakes come
and the mountains crumble into the sea.
Let the oceans roar and foam.
Let the mountains tremble as the waters surge!
"Be still, and know that I am God!
I will be honored by every nation.
I will be honored throughout the world."
The Lord of Heaven's Armies is here among us;
the God of Israel is our fortress.

What's the point?
If you're going through trouble today, don't be afraid of it. God hasn't left you. He's working behind the scenes to make sure events unfold the way that's best for you.

He knows what He's doing. Sometimes it may feel like we're trapped in the middle. It may feel like He's dropped the ball. And it's absolutely tempting to give up. But resist the urge to strike out on your own. Trust Him.

March 24

God is exalted in our stillness

IF YOU ARE a Christ-follower, at some point in your walk with God, you've run yourself into the ground trying to make Him happy. Christians have this idea that we need to work ourselves to death in order to exalt God's name, but the truth is that God doesn't need us to do that. His name will be exalted regardless of us.

Psalm 46:10
"Be still, and know that I am God!
I will be honored by every nation.
I will be honored throughout the world."

God will be exalted whether we work for Him or not. He will be exalted whether we acknowledge Him or not. I mean, for Pete's sake, even rocks rejoice and give Him praise. He doesn't need us to. He wants us to. He wants to have a relationship with us more than anything, but He doesn't need us to be exalted.

God doesn't say to stress to yourself out so He can be exalted. He says be still, know He's God, and He'll take care of it.

What's the point?
Maybe God has called you to do something, and that's great. And you should do your best. But He never calls you to run yourself into the ground to make Him happy.

So stop stressing out. Be still. Know God. He'll be exalted. And actually, He will be exalted more in your stillness than He would have been in your stress.

March 25

Walking in the storm with Jesus

CHRISTIANS HAVE THIS idea that if we're following Jesus we won't have to go through difficult times, but I'm not sure where we get that idea. The Bible tells us over and over again that Jesus will be with us in the storms of our life, but it never says that He'll calm them first.

Matthew 14:24-27
Meanwhile, the disciples were in trouble far away from land, for a strong wind had risen, and they were fighting heavy waves. About three o'clock in the morning Jesus came toward them, walking on the water. When the disciples saw him walking on the water, they were terrified. In their fear, they cried out, "It's a ghost!" But Jesus spoke to them at once. "Don't be afraid," he said. "Take courage. I am here!"

It's interesting to me that Jesus didn't calm the storm from the shore. No. He walked out to them in the storm, met them where they were, and then stayed in sight throughout the storm until He decided it was time for it to stop.

What's the point?
We may have to go deeper into the storms of our life before God chooses to calm them. But as long as we keep our eyes on Him, we won't sink.

Don't forget that He's there. Don't get so overwhelmed with your troubles that you think He isn't right there with you. Remind yourself that He has walked out into the storms of your life to stand with you in your darkest moments. And when you can see Him, don't take your eyes off Him.

March 26

Worry and stress are bread and butter

IT'S EASY TO worry about the stuff we can't control, but it's exhausting. It's an emotional roller coaster, and it doesn't accomplish anything. But somehow worry and stress have become the two mainstays of the American emotional diet. Worry and stress are our bread and butter, and we have this idea that if we aren't worried or stressed about something, we aren't working hard enough.

Matthew 6:31-33
"So don't worry about these things, saying, 'What will we eat? What will we drink? What will we wear?' These things dominate the thoughts of unbelievers, but your heavenly Father already knows all your needs. Seek the Kingdom of God above all else, and live righteously, and he will give you everything you need."

Worry is a waste of time. You can worry all you like, and it won't change a single thing about your situation. I work and worry and stress myself out to accomplish the things I think I need to accomplish, and most of my stress and anxiety comes from those self-inflicted deadlines. But are those the things I need? I think I need them. But God is the one who knows for sure.

What's the point?
God knows what I need, and He's a good God. He won't withhold something out of spite. Worrying about what you don't have runs you dry of emotion and energy, and it doesn't accomplish anything.

Do what God wants. Live for Him. Let the rest go. You'll enjoy life more, and He'll accomplish great things through you.

March 27

Worry is like a short cut in Houston

I WAS BORN in Houston. It's full of people, smog, and cars, and you haven't experienced traffic until you've driven there. Growing up there, my mom had to drive us around, and I remember sitting in the backseat on multiple occasions when Mom announced that we were going to take a shortcut.

That was my cue to beg her not to, because her shortcuts never worked. We'd always end up more lost than we started.

And that's kind of what it's like when you choose to worry instead of pray.

John 14:27
"I am leaving you with a gift—peace of mind and heart. And the peace I give is a gift the world cannot give. So don't be troubled or afraid."

This is Jesus consoling His disciples shortly before His death. He didn't want them to worry because He knew it would only distract them from the great plans He had for them.

Worry strips us of our effectiveness, and yet we all still cling to it because we've given into this cultural lie that it helps us do more. But worry is like taking a shortcut in Houston – it's stressful, complicated, and you never end up where you think you should be.

What's the point?
You can choose to worry, or you can choose to pray. Praying about your problem means you give it to God. Worrying about it means you keep it for yourself, and you'll keep coming back to it over and over again.

It may be easier to worry, but it will ultimately cost you more time and energy and effort than you have. Just like a shortcut in Houston.

March 30

You can claim overwhelming victory

DO YOU SEE yourself as a winner, or have you bought into the world's lie that you're a loser? If you are a follower of Christ, there's something you need to know before you walk out your door in the morning.

Romans 8:35-37
Can anything ever separate us from Christ's love? Does it mean he no longer loves us if we have trouble or calamity, or are persecuted, or hungry, or destitute, or in danger, or threatened with death? (As the Scriptures say, "For your sake we are killed every day; we are being slaughtered like sheep.") No, despite all these things, overwhelming victory is ours through Christ, who loved us.

Overwhelming victory? Did you see that? Losers don't get to claim overwhelming victory, and that's what God says is ours through the power of Jesus Christ.

It's one thing to know that overwhelming victory is yours through Christ. It's something else to acknowledge that such a thing is possible. But it's something else entirely to live like it's truth. Because if you believe it, there is no chance, no risk, no danger because overwhelming victory is already yours through Christ.

What's the point?
Whatever you're facing today, you don't have to do it in your own strength. Don't try to win with your charm or your intelligence. Don't try to gain victory with your money or your influence.

If you want to win, if you want victory, turn to Christ. He's your secret weapon. Through Him, you can do anything. Through Him, you can more than conquer. You can live.

March 31

Today is a gift

A FRIEND OF MINE once told me that life is like a war and every day is a battle that we win or lose. Every day is a new opportunity to either do something for God or to focus on ourselves, and it's up to us to choose.

Psalm 118:24
This is the day the Lord has made. We will rejoice and be glad in it.

It's easy for me to get into a rut thinking that life just happens. I'm a creature of habit, so for me to keep up with all the craziness of my life, I have to develop habits in repeatable patterns. Otherwise I forget things. But as a result of building habits into a lifestyle, I get to thinking that every day just happens. And that's not the case.

Every day is a gift.

It's one more chance to do something awesome for God. It's one more chance for God to do something amazing through us. And no matter what happened yesterday and no matter what you have planned for tomorrow, today is the day God wants you to live right now.

What's the point?
We can choose to make today a new day, or we can choose to make today just like any other day. Not that living a day like any other day is bad, but if we can remember that every day is a gift, maybe we will change our perspective a little. Because we can worship God with our habits, just like we can worship Him in spontaneity.

So be thankful for the day you have today.

April 2015

FOLLOWING GOD

Choosing to follow Christ is a lifetime commitment, and it's not an easy one. It's definitely worth it, but if you're expecting that you'll always understand where you're going, you need to think again. God's thoughts and ways are higher than ours, but even though He doesn't always make sense, we have to keep following.

April 1
Stop thinking you know better

SOMETIMES I FEEL like I'm wandering through life without a plan, and that frustrates the dickens out of me because I like plans. I like maps. I like knowing the big picture so I know how badly I can screw up before I ruin everything.

But the truth is that nobody knows the big picture. Only God knows that, and that's why He has promised to guide us.

Isaiah 58:11
The Lord will guide you continually,
giving you water when you are dry
and restoring your strength.
You will be like a well-watered garden,
like an ever-flowing spring.

What I have learned is that walking with God isn't about rules and regulations and rituals that only have symbolic meaning and no real life application. Following God isn't about being good or following the rules or putting on a good Christian show. It's about living life with Him. It's about living and loving the way He does.

God never stops guiding us. He never stops leading us. If we get turned around, it's because we took someone else's directions. But God's still on the path. He's still waiting for us to turn around and go back to where He is.

What's the point?
If you've gotten off the path, go back. If you haven't left, don't leave. Just keep following where He's leading you, and along the way, you won't lack anything you need. In fact, he'll continuously provide, not just for your basic needs but strength to conquer the challenges too.

April 2

Can you trust what your eyes tell you

MY BROTHER AND I were out eating one evening, and the waiter came up behind us and said, "Good evening, ladies!"

My brother has long hair, by the way. And a beard. But the waiter only saw him from behind and made a bad assumption based on what he could see.

Hebrews 11:1-3
Faith is the confidence that what we hope for will actually happen; it gives us assurance about things we cannot see. Through their faith, the people in days of old earned a good reputation. By faith we understand that the entire universe was formed at God's command, that what we now see did not come from anything that can be seen.

You can't always trust what your eyes are telling you. Sometimes your eyes will tell you something true, like whether or not the light is on or off, but other times your eyes tell you things you have to interpret based on your opinions and your perspective. Then, to know the truth, you have to know the whole story.

It's not wrong to question, of course, but don't make judgment calls based on half the story. Otherwise you'll be the waiter who calls a man a woman.

What's the point?
God has told us what we can expect from Him. Don't put words in His mouth.

The next time you're tempted to make an assumption about God (or your neighbor or anyone really) based on something you've seen, think twice. You don't see the whole picture.

April 3

Something small can change the world

FINISHING PROJECTS MAKES me happy. But have you ever done something that succeeded beyond your expectations? Have you ever completed a project that made a difference far beyond what you had planned?

Yes, sometimes success is a result of our hard work. Our hard work certainly contributes to it. But there are other times in life that my success has less to do with how hard I've worked and more to do with how God uses the work I've done.

Ephesians 3:20
Now all glory to God, who is able, through his mighty power at work within us, to accomplish infinitely more than we might ask or think.

If you're a Christ-follower, everything you do for other people, no matter how small, can grow to become something God can use to change a life. And that's not something that happens on its own or because of you; it's God working through you that makes the difference.

We don't have the power on our own to change anything, to accomplish anything of great significance, to heal the hurting or the find the lost. All of that is outside the realm of our ability, but God can do it through us every day. With God, those small acts of kindness become big heart-changing victories. With God, the tiniest deed done in His name can endure for a lifetime.

What's the point?
Dream big and don't be afraid to do something for God.

He can take your tiny little achievements and use them to influence people for ages and ages to come.

April 6

No excuses

HAS GOD EVER asked you to do something you don't have time for? Maybe it's a ministry or service for someone. Whatever it is, you look at your calendar and you just know there's no way you can make it happen. But you also know there's no denying He's telling you to do it.

What do you do?

Joshua 10:12-14
On the day the Lord gave the Israelites victory over the Amorites, Joshua prayed to the Lord in front of all the people of Israel. He said, "Let the sun stand still over Gibeon, and the moon over the valley of Aijalon." So the sun stood still and the moon stayed in place until the nation of Israel had defeated its enemies. Is this event not recorded in The Book of Jashar? The sun stayed in the middle of the sky, and it did not set as on a normal day. There has never been a day like this one before or since, when the Lord answered such a prayer. Surely the Lord fought for Israel that day!

Yes, you read that right. The sun and moon stood still so Israel would have the time to defeat their enemies. God stopped time itself.

What's the point?
If God has told you to do something, He doesn't expect you to carry out His plans on your own strength. Granted, He may not stop the sun and moon, but He will make a way somehow.

God will help you achieve the plans He has for you. You aren't on your own, so stop living like it. No more excuses.

April 7

Everybody needs to laugh more

WHEN WAS THE last time you laughed until your sides hurt? You know the kind of laughter I mean. The loud, unrestrained, perfectly jolly laughter that you just can't stop. Have you ever laughed that hard? I recommend it.

Proverbs 17:22
A cheerful heart is good medicine,
but a broken spirit saps a person's strength.

We all need to laugh more. We all take life so seriously all the time, and Christians are the worst about this. We focus on the doom and gloom. We focus on everything that's wrong in the world, wrong in our lives, wrong in other people's lives. And I'm not saying we're wrong, necessarily. But I am saying that we seriously need to lighten up.

What's the point?

It's important to be serious about things you need to be serious about, but in turn you are allowed to be silly about silly things. You can relax and have fun. Or do you think God giving you a sense of humor was an accident? Do you think the gift of laughter just happened?

No way. We need to laugh. Spend time laughing, and you'll see a difference in your entire perspective.

Give yourself permission to play. Go outside. Have fun. Run around. Be a kid again. Don't worry about what's coming tomorrow. Don't fret over what happened yesterday. Just enjoy having a relationship with your Daddy, and if something funny happens, don't hesitate to laugh yourself into an asthma attack. Once you can breathe again, you'll be glad you did.

April 8

Where do you go for help?

WHEN YOU NEED help where do you look? Do you read an instruction manual? Do you Google the problem? When I have a problem I don't know how to solve, my first instinct is to find a way to solve it on my own. I rarely ask for advice.

And there's nothing wrong with trying to find the answer on your own, but what happens when nobody can help? Where do you go then?

Psalm 121:1-2
I look up to the mountains—
does my help come from there?
My help comes from the Lord,
who made heaven and earth!

How often do we just sit down and ask God for help? God has all the answers we need, and we have access to everything we need through Him. So why do we try to fix things on our own? For me, I don't like relying on anyone. I don't like being dependent on anyone else. But I'm not self-sufficient, as much as my pride tells me I am.

What's the point?
When you need answers, that's when you turn to the Bible, God's Word to everyone. It has the answers we need for the problems we're facing, how to live, how to work, how to love.

Are you trying to figure out life's issues on your own? You can try, but you're going to hit a dead end when your knowledge runs out. That's why God's Word is everything—because it never runs out of wisdom.

April 9
Life is a missions trip

THE FASTEST WAY to adapt to a new culture is to jump in and start living in it. Nothing will help you learn a new language and culture faster than potential starvation.

The longer you live in a different culture than the one you were born in, the easier it becomes to fit in. Most times, that's great, but what if the culture you're moving into rejects God completely? How do you live in it without turning your back on God?

Colossians 2:8
Don't let anyone capture you with empty philosophies and high-sounding nonsense that come from human thinking and from the spiritual powers of this world, rather than from Christ.

We are surrounded every moment by the faith systems of our world. And because we are surrounded by them constantly — on television and radio and the internet and even our closest friends — it's easy to adopt their perspective. But the moment you agree to see things their way, you're opening the door to let the culture take over.

What's the point?
Don't just switch off your brain and accept everything you hear on television or on the radio or on the internet. Don't just accept everything you hear at church. Don't just accept everything your good Christian friends tell you.

If you belong to Christ, this world isn't your home. So this culture isn't your home either. Question everything. And if the answers contradict Scripture, if the answers you find go against what Christ has said, don't believe them. And if you can't understand them, trust God to work it out.

April 10

Let God into your life

I STRUGGLE WITH going God's way sometimes because I want to go my way. With my way, I can see how the path twists and turns. At least, I think I can. Of course, when difficult times come my way, my plan turns out to be pretty much useless.

What's nice about going God's way is that He really does know all the pitfalls along the path you're walking. He doesn't have just some half-baked idea on how to survive when life gets tough. God knows everything about the road He asks us to take.

Psalm 18:30
God's way is perfect.
All the Lord's promises prove true.
He is a shield for all who look to him for protection.

If you don't ever give God a chance — a real, honest chance — you will never understand who He is. And I'm not talking about a half-hearted attempt. Even Christians can fall prey to this.

We're all so comfortable in our Christian churches and our Christian homes, listening to Christian radio, watching Christian TV and going to Christian movies. We're so caught up in "being Christian," we have forgotten what it means to follow Christ.

What's the point?
Give God a chance. Follow His way for a little while. Trust in one of His promises. Seek shelter under His wings during a difficult day. Believe Him. He's waiting for us to open our eyes and accept the relationship He's been offering for all our lives.

April 13

God will work out his plans for us

EVERYBODY'S LIFE TURNS upside down at one point or another. Everyone has been abandoned and betrayed by friends. Everyone has sometimes wondered where God went. And I know we sometimes wonder just what the heck God is doing.

But then I remember that if I could always understand the way God thinks, He wouldn't be God.

Psalm 138:8
The Lord will work out his plans for my life—
for your faithful love, O Lord, endures forever.
Don't abandon me, for you made me.

God has plans for my life. And He's got plans for your life too, even though it may not feel like it now. What I struggle with the most is feeling like nothing is happening, feeling like all I'm doing is waiting, like the only thing I accomplish in a day is converting oxygen into CO_2.

But the truth is that God is the one who works life out. Not us.

What's the point?
All I have to do is wait and listen and be ready to move. When God tells me to do something, I need to do it no matter how crazy it might sound because when He asks me to do something it's going to be a part of His plan for my life.

When I'm moving in tandem with God's plan, that's when He can start to accomplish huge things that I would never have been able to do on my own.

April 14
Unity

IF YOU WANT a good time, lock two Christians in a room together and see what happens. I'm pretty sure there will be fireworks within the hour.

Why? Because Christians can be the hardest people in the world to get along with. And most of the time we don't even agree with each other.

I don't think most Christians intentionally mean to create conflict with each other. I do think Satan plays a hand in some of it, but a lot of it has to do with the way we treat each other.

Romans 15:5-6
May God, who gives this patience and encouragement, help you live in complete harmony with each other, as is fitting for followers of Christ Jesus. Then all of you can join together with one voice, giving praise and glory to God, the Father of our Lord Jesus Christ.

Sounds like even the Christians in early Rome had trouble getting along. This verse just points out the reason why we all need to work together.

God left us here for a purpose. He's got something for us to do, otherwise we wouldn't still be here.

What's the point?
So instead of picking on each other, instead of only seeing each other's faults and failures, instead of focusing on why we don't like each other, let's live in harmony together. Those of us who follow Christ should love each other, forgive each other, make allowances for each other's faults, because Lord knows we have enough faults of our own.

If we can all get along, who knows what God can do through us?

April 15

Sweet water from a bitter well

IF WE NEED advice from someone, we usually go looking for the most qualified person in that field to find the answers we need. If we need legal counsel, we look for a successful lawyer. If we need car advice, we look for a successful mechanic. If we need advice on how to get somewhere, we ask someone who's been there or someone who at least knows the area.

So when we need advice on how to live our lives, why do we look to the world?

James 3:17-18
But the wisdom from above is first of all pure. It is also peace loving, gentle at all times, and willing to yield to others. It is full of mercy and good deeds. It shows no favoritism and is always sincere. And those who are peacemakers will plant seeds of peace and reap a harvest of righteousness.

The world embraces a way of life that provides temporary happiness but no long-lasting satisfaction. That's where God's way is different. When you start following God, you will not always be happy. And that's just the beginning. It gets harder. It gets harder and harder and harder to follow God. But the longer you follow Him, the more He makes His faithfulness known to you.

What's the point?
Following the world's wisdom will leave you nothing but emptiness inside. Maybe it doesn't seem like following Jesus is such a good idea at first, but it doesn't take long for you to understand that even though you have nothing, God has given you everything.

April 16

Jump when God says so

HAVE YOU EVER walked away from an open door? I have. Lots of times. God has dropped opportunities in my lap, and I've passed them by for one reason or another. Fear or anxiety. Uncertainty or insecurity. Laziness is one too. Sometimes it's because I wasn't paying close enough attention to recognize it in the first place.

Genesis 12:1-4
The Lord had said to Abram, "Leave your native country, your relatives, and your father's family, and go to the land that I will show you. I will make you into a great nation. I will bless you and make you famous, and you will be a blessing to others. I will bless those who bless you and curse those who treat you with contempt. All the families on earth will be blessed through you." So Abram departed as the Lord had instructed, and Lot went with him. Abram was seventy-five years old when he left Haran.

Put yourself in Abram's (also known as Abraham) shoes. Would you have done what he did? He left everything he knew because God spoke to him.

Abram made the choice to believe Him. And not only did Abram believe, he acted.

What's the point?
Don't miss the opportunities He gives you. Don't ignore them because you're afraid of them or because you aren't sure you're talented enough.

God doesn't open a door for no reason. No, it might not lead the way we want it to, but if it's a path God has opened, it's worth traveling.

April 17

Living for what you have to leave behind

WHAT DO WE take with us when we die? Not our money or our homes, not our possessions or our status. We take our own soul. That's it. And if you're fortunate and very blessed, you won't have to go alone. You'll get to go home with your friends and your family members. And those are the treasures that really matter.

Psalm 84:10
A single day in your courts
is better than a thousand anywhere else!
I would rather be a gatekeeper in the house of my God
than live the good life in the homes of the wicked.

If we look at heaven as our home and Earth as our college dorm or as our rental house, it changes the way you look at a lot of things. You can't hang pictures in a leased apartment. Or at least, you probably shouldn't. In a home you know is temporary, you shouldn't invest a lot of time changing it because you know you are going to leave. Instead, use your time to invest in the things that last, like the people who live around you.

What's the point?
Our world would have us believe that gaining wealth on Earth is our purpose here, but you can't take that kind of wealth with you when you die.

We need to get our perspective straight. Do you believe that a day in God's presence is better than a lifetime on Earth? Would you rather be the lowliest servant in God's house than a wealthy person here?

Make up your mind.

April 20

Being bullied is a privilege

THE WORLD IS full of bullies in all shapes and sizes too. They aren't just thugs who are after your lunch money anymore. A bully is anyone who uses any kind of intimidation to get what he or she wants. They are in offices and homes and on the street, and they aren't always physical.

So how do you handle bullies when you're a grown up?

Philippians 1:28-29
Don't be intimidated in any way by your enemies. This will be a sign to them that they are going to be destroyed, but that you are going to be saved, even by God himself. For you have been given not only the privilege of trusting in Christ but also the privilege of suffering for him.

Suffering for Christ is an honor. Have you ever thought about it that way? Whenever I hear the phrase suffering for Christ, I think of the oppressed and persecuted Christians in Asia and the Middle East. That's suffering. But being intimidated by a passive-aggressive bully and choosing not to strike back is suffering too.

What's the point?

When you choose not to strike back and trust God instead, you're doing that for the glory of God. You're suffering for Christ. I know it doesn't feel like a privilege when you're being emotionally raked over the coals, but that's what it is.

Don't be intimidated by those who would tear you down just so they can get what they want. Stand your ground lovingly in the name of Christ, and watch what God does as a result.

April 21

Succeed or fail, victory comes from God

DO YOU EVER just have upsetting days? Those days where everything conspires against you to ruin your mood? When that happens, how do you calm down?

When you're so angry, you can't even speak–when you're so frustrated, it's all you can do not to burst into tears–how do you see God in that situation?

Psalm 62:1-2
I wait quietly before God,
for my victory comes from him.
He alone is my rock and my salvation,
my fortress where I will never be shaken.

Making hasty decisions is always a bad idea. And making hasty decisions when you're angry will always, always make more trouble than it solves.

I want to run. I want to fight. But all I'm supposed to do is to wait quietly before God because my victory comes from Him. Sure, that may mean I need to make some changes. But that doesn't mean I have to take it all on my own shoulders and make decisions on my own.

But what it does mean–for now? I need to remember where my hope is. Not in people. Not in the world. But in my God.

What's the point?
Are you angry today? Frustrated? Lost and unsure of yourself or what you're supposed to do? Instead of scrambling to make sense of it or to defend yourself or to find an answer, think about just waiting quietly before God. Stand still and be open to what He wants, instead of just what you want.

April 22

What questions should you not ask God?

EVERYBODY HAS QUESTIONS for God. Sometimes they're silly. Sometimes they're serious. But every now and then, you end up in a situation where you need an answer. You have to make a decision, and you can only put it off for so long. You have to choose.

James 1:5
If you need wisdom, ask our generous God, and he will give it to you. He will not rebuke you for asking.

So many times I think we are afraid to ask God because bringing our daily concerns to Him seems trivial. I mean, He's God. He shouldn't care about the simple, easy, picky things I'm facing in my life. But that's a lie. He does.

God wants to be a part of our lives in every way, from the big decisions to the small ones. We should never forget that even small decisions can have huge consequences, so it's essential to ask for wisdom before you make any decision.

What's the point?
Don't let Satan's lies convince you that your problem isn't worth God's time. That's not your decision to make. You've been invited to ask; so ask. And don't believe for a second that you have life handled on your own, because you don't. Nobody does.

Just ask. Be sure about what you need to know. Trust that God will give you an answer. And then be willing to act on it, whether it makes sense to your friends and family or not.

April 23

Making God a priority is an attitude

LIFE IS ALWAYS busy, and I find myself constantly embroiled in a conflict between priorities. I remember being told that God should be my priority. Period. Nothing should come before Him, and I agree with that and believe it.

But what does that look like? And how do I juggle all the other responsibilities I have with that one priority? Making God the priority in life has to be practical somehow, otherwise we couldn't do it. Right?

Matthew 6:33
Seek the Kingdom of God above all else, and live righteously, and he will give you everything you need.

When we face choices in life, seeking God first means doing what the Bible says is right and listening to the Holy Spirit's voice and obeying. But what I've learned is that it's not always what choice you make. It's why you make it.

What's the point?
Seeking God first, making God a priority, is an attitude. If everything you do is for the glory of God, every choice you make will reflect that.

So stop worrying about what choice you're going to make and focus instead on the why behind it. Look at your motivation. Is it out of fear or worry or pride or anger? If you're making a choice for any reason other than God's glory, you aren't putting Him first.

We all face choices every moment of every day, and God has given us everything we need to make the wise choice. So do it.

April 24

Believing God will do as He promised

WHEN SOMEONE PROMISES to do something for me, generally that means I have to sit back and wait for them to make good on that promise. It's hard to sit still when your future is on the line. It's hard to sit still and keep waiting on somebody else's actions when you have the opportunity to make something happen yourself.

So what happens when the person you're waiting on is God?

Hebrews 6:11-12
Our great desire is that you will keep on loving others as long as life lasts, in order to make certain that what you hope for will come true. Then you will not become spiritually dull and indifferent. Instead, you will follow the example of those who are going to inherit God's promises because of their faith and endurance.

Following God is a process. God never says it's anything other than that. Following Christ takes faith, and faith takes a strange combination of hard work and patience.

God will never ask you to do something He won't equip you for. Maybe He'll equip you along the way. Maybe He's equipped you already, and you just don't know it.

What's the point?
It's not your job to worry about how you're going to meet your financial needs. It's your job to make sure you're doing what God has called you to do, and God will take care of your needs.

We just have to believe that God will do what He's promised (that's faith) and hold on until the plan comes together (that's endurance).

April 27

Grace when we make mistakes

I HATE MAKING mistakes, and I'm the first one to suggest punishment once I have screwed up. But what do you do when you make a mistake and no one punishes you?

Ephesians 2:4-9
But God is so rich in mercy, and he loved us so much, that even though we were dead because of our sins, he gave us life when he raised Christ from the dead. (It is only by God's grace that you have been saved!) For he raised us from the dead along with Christ and seated us with him in the heavenly realms because we are united with Christ Jesus. So God can point to us in all future ages as examples of the incredible wealth of his grace and kindness toward us, as shown in all he has done for us who are united with Christ Jesus. God saved you by his grace when you believed. And you can't take credit for this; it is a gift from God. Salvation is not a reward for the good things we have done, so none of us can boast about it.

The truth about God is this: God forgives us for so much more than mistakes. God forgives us for sin.

We deserve death. We deserve Hell. But God wouldn't let us face the consequences without giving us a choice. Never forget what Jesus had to go through so we could have a choice.

What's the point?
Don't forget what grace means to you and never hesitate to extend it to someone else.

Nobody deserves it, but God hands it out freely. So we should too.

April 28

Every family has responsibilities

IN EVERY FAMILY, each member has a responsibility. Sort of like in a body, where every part has something it's designed to do. When I was little and my family would go camping, each one of us had an assigned job at the campsite, and it was our responsibility to do our part, otherwise things just didn't get done. So when we choose to join the family of God, why do we think it's any different?

Luke 12:48
When someone has been given much, much will be required in return; and when someone has been entrusted with much, even more will be required.

If you're a Christian who was raised in a godly home, who had access to a Bible from the earliest days of your youth, who had parents who taught you to respect God and love Him, who had a church that encouraged you to grow in maturity, you haven't just been given much. You've been entrusted with much.

There are no accidents. There are no coincidences.

What's the point?
If you grew up in a Christian home, if you've known Christ since you were a child, and you aren't actively involved in serving others today, you're in trouble. Because you're part of a family. You're part of God's family. And you have a responsibility to that family.

You've been entrusted with the greatest responsibility there is– loving people, helping people meet Christ–and if you throw it away or ignore it because it makes you uncomfortable or because it's too much work, God is going to have something to say about that.

April 29

We are already victorious

DO YOU EVER feel stuck? Like nothing you accomplish actually helps you move forward? You can work your hardest and try with all your might, but you still don't seem to be going anywhere. You're just stuck. You just have to wait. And I hate being in that place. I feel helpless and useless. I feel like I can't do anything right, and I feel like nothing is ever going to change.

Exodus 15:2
The Lord is my strength and my song;
he has given me victory.
This is my God, and I will praise him—
my father's God, and I will exalt him!

We give the Israelites in the Bible such a hard time for turning against God whenever they had the chance, but what do we do? God has done the same (if not more) for us, and we still have days where we ask Him where He is.

Like so many things in life, the issue is perspective. God has already won the victory over death and sin. He's already conquered all the real enemies in our lives. So why be upset? Why be discouraged? Why be frustrated?

What's the point?

This life won't always go the way you want it to, but don't be like the Israelites, who praised God for His goodness one moment and then complained about His plan the next.

God has given us victory. Period. It may not always look like we want it to, but it's not up to us anyway.

April 30
Living all in

COMMITMENT IS ONE of the scariest words in the English language. It means you're making a promise to see it through to the end. Commitment takes hard work and loyalty and lots and lots of grace, both received and extended, and whether it's a person, a goal, or a cause, you won't see the end of that promise overnight.

1 Kings 8:61
And may you be completely faithful to the Lord our God. May you always obey his decrees and commands, just as you are doing today.

You can make a promise to someone or you can promise to achieve something without putting your whole heart and soul into it. You can make a half-hearted commitment, and it's safer that way. Because that way when people hurt you or when people let you down or when situations don't work out the way you expect them to, you can protect yourself from disappointment.

But there's nothing about that lifestyle that says completely faithful is there? There's nothing whole about that method of commitment at all. And maybe you protect yourself by only committing half of your heart, but, in the end, you only reap half the reward.

What's the point?
We're not called to live a half-life. We're called to live all in. So stop hoarding your chips. Push them all to the center of the table and let God take over the game.

I won't say it'll be easy, and I can't promise that you won't have trouble, but I can tell you that God's holding all the cards anyway. So who would you rather bet on?

May 2015

WHAT REALLY MATTERS

Jesus spent a lot of time talking about the things in life that really matter when He was on Earth. There are a lot of places throughout the Bible where Jesus shared wisdom with His followers. There are also a lot of places where His followers, like the Apostle Paul, applied God's definition of what matters to life.

We need to learn to do the same. Otherwise, we'll forever be trapped in the downward spiral of living our lives for the things that don't matter. And that's the fastest route to discouragement.

✓ May 1

Knowing what matters when life is busy

BEING BUSY ISN'T always bad, but good or bad, busyness alters your perspective. In the heat of the moment, in that panicked second where you have to make an immediate decision, sometimes we choose based on what we think is important at that very instant.

The best way to handle those panicked moments is to identify what matters first before those moments come.

Philippians 1:9-11
I pray that your love will overflow more and more, and that you will keep on growing in knowledge and understanding. For I want you to understand what really matters, so that you may live pure and blameless lives until the day of Christ's return. May you always be filled with the fruit of your salvation—the righteous character produced in your life by Jesus Christ—for this will bring much glory and praise to God.

This is what I want for my life. I want to love people in a way that makes a difference in their lives, and I want to be able focus on the things that are truly important. And if I can do that, I can live a life that points people to Christ instead of away from Him.

What's the point?
Paul prayed that the Philippians would understand what mattered in their lives, and that sounds like a pretty good place to start. After all, if we never ask, there's a chance we'll never know.

So if you want to know what matters in your life, start off by asking God to show you. He's listening.

✓ May 4
Love God, love people

WHEN I TRY to focus on the things that matter in my life, my brain instantly goes to the rules. I'm a performance-driven perfectionist, so I actually like rules. I'm not a big fan of breaking them either.

So even though I know that the rules don't make me righteous (only Christ can do that), I still want to follow them because if God hadn't given them, they wouldn't be important. But which rules matter most?

Matthew 22:36-40
"Teacher, which is the most important commandment in the law of Moses?"
Jesus replied, "'You must love the Lord your God with all your heart, all your soul, and all your mind.' This is the first and greatest commandment. A second is equally important: 'Love your neighbor as yourself.' The entire law and all the demands of the prophets are based on these two commandments."

I love that Christ summarizes the Law in two concepts. Love God. Love people.

It's basic, but it's real. And it's true. If you love God and love people, your entire outlook on life will change. That doesn't mean it's easy. Loving God isn't hard, of course. He's God, and He's wonderful. But loving people? That's a challenge.

What's the point?
Jesus says the most important things to remember about following Him are to love God and love people. As Christ-followers, we need to make up our mind to live that way.

Maybe people make you angry. Just remember that they need the same amount of grace that you did.

✓ May 5
Do right

I'VE ONLY SEEN a message in the clouds once. I can't remember what the airplane was writing with the smoke against the blue sky, but I remember seeing it and wondering why God couldn't make His instructions so clear.

Do you ever feel that way? Do you ever wish that God would just tell you what He expects of you?

Micah 6:8
No, O people, the Lord has told you what is good,
and this is what he requires of you:
to do what is right, to love mercy,
and to walk humbly with your God.

It honestly doesn't get much clearer than that, does it? Do what's right. Love mercy. Walk humbly. But hang on a second. Think about those three things. What do they actually mean? What is God actually telling us to do?

Let's take it one concept at a time. Do what is right.

The beginning of the verse says that God has told us what is good. So now He expects us to do it. Can you be a Christ-follower and not do what's right? Sure. But why would you want to?

What's the point?
Read the Bible and learn what is right, and then focus on doing it every day. Eventually doing what's right will become a habit, and it's a good habit to have because just as poor choices have bad consequences, good choices eventually have great rewards.

Do what's right. That matters to God, so it should matter to us.

✓ May 6
Love mercy

WHEN SOMEONE WRONGS you, how do you respond? It feels right to reciprocate when someone does wrong to us, but it's not the way we're supposed to live. And it's not what God expects from us.

Micah 6:8
No, O people, the Lord has told you what is good,
and this is what he requires of you:
to do what is right, to love mercy,
and to walk humbly with your God.

I don't have any problem loving people who are good to me. It's the buttheads I struggle with.

God gives us mercy every day. I mean, unless you're perfect all the time, you need mercy every hour. I do. And if I loved mercy like I was supposed to, I would jump at the opportunity to forgive someone when they hurt me. Loving mercy is being kind especially to the people who don't deserve our kindness.

Granted, you shouldn't waste your effort and energy investing in someone who is just going to turn around and attack you. But whether they attack you or not, whether they waste your time or not, you can still be kind in your dealings with them. And that's what it means to love mercy.

What's the point?
Focus on being kind to people, especially if they don't deserve it. Look for opportunities to extend mercy to people around you, and be brave enough to tell them why.

Be willing to explain that your mercy comes in Jesus' name. Who knows? Understanding that might change more than their attitude. It could change their whole life.

✅ May 7
Walk humbly

WHEN LIFE GETS complicated, sometimes it's good to go back to the basics. I don't know why the basics are often the first thing we forget, but when life turns upside-down or gets so packed full of responsibility, there's something in me that wants to twist off and just make things up as I go.

We don't need to make up a new answer. Most of the time, the answer's already in front of us.

Micah 6:8
No, O people, the Lord has told you what is good,
and this is what he requires of you:
to do what is right, to love mercy,
and to walk humbly with your God.

When the Bible talks about walking, usually it means living in general. So this is saying that we need to live humbly, but is humility selling everything you own and living in poverty? Is it never saying anything positive about yourself? I don't think so.

What's the point?
Humility is more than just giving away your possessions or choosing to live in poverty. Like faith, humility is a lifestyle. It's not just one choice you make; it's a series of choices flowing from the attitude of your heart. And that heart attitude comes from understanding who God is and how He sees you.

Pride is trying to be the boss of your own life. Humility is accepting that God knows better than you do.

Live humbly. Let God have the wheel.

✓ May 8

We already depend on God

IF YOU'VE BEEN following Christ for any amount of time, you'll recognize pretty quickly that the way we are supposed to think, to live, and to see ourselves is completely opposite from what the world says.

Matthew 5:3
God blesses those who are poor and realize their need for him, for the Kingdom of Heaven is theirs.

Those who are poor and need God are blessed. Wow. Isn't that the opposite of everything we are taught? But think about what a life entirely dependent on God would look like. We wouldn't need to find our identity somewhere else. We wouldn't need to find happiness anywhere else.

So why don't we all live that way? God already gives us everything we need. Air to breathe. Food to eat. I'm already 100% dependent on Him, but if I refuse to acknowledge it, I'll never be satisfied.

What's the point?
God has already provided everything I need. The one place where the whole thing breaks down is me—my attitude about Him. Attitude is everything, and until I acknowledge how much I need Him, I'm going to keep on worrying, keep on fighting, keep on struggling, keep on envying, etc. etc. etc. And that's not the way we're supposed to live.

Acknowledge your insignificance. Once you get past the roadblock of pride and realize how much you need Him, something changes in your thinking.

We weren't designed to live on our own. We were designed for life with Christ. And until we accept that, we'll never stop searching.

✓ May 11

God expects us to mourn

WHAT HAVE YOU lost? A job? An opportunity? A friend? Everyone loses. Loss is just part of life, and learning how to deal with loss is part of growing up.

For the first time since 1965, Wichita State University made it to the 2013 NCAA Final Four Championship. I'm not a sports fan, but I am a Shocker. I bought a t-shirt, and I even watched the game. And while it was a great game, it didn't turn out the way I hoped. They lost, yes, but they'll recover. They'll come back stronger than before.

What about significant losses? Losing a game is one thing you can recover from. Losing a person you loved?

Matthew 5:4
God blesses those who mourn,
for they will be comforted.

When you are mourning–and I'm talking about a significant loss, not a basketball game–when the grief is just too much for you to bear, that is a true expression of sadness, and that isn't wrong. God expects us to mourn. There's a time for it. But as a Christ follower, we can have a different perspective than those who don't believe, because we know God.

Mourning is a season of sadness, yes, but as Christ-followers we can understand that seasons pass and God is still faithful.

What's the point?
If you are suffering through a time of sadness right now, don't be afraid to show it. Mourning doesn't make you a bad Christian. It just gives you the opportunity to receive comfort from the God who loves you no matter what.

✓ May 12
Watch out for the quiet ones

SOME DAYS I get tired of being quiet. Some days I want to fight and argue and lash out at everyone who has hurt me, but reacting that way rarely solves the problem. And it just gets worse and worse until someone backs down.

Yes, there are some things in life we should stand up for, but do we have to fight to make a difference?

Matthew 5:5
God blesses those who are humble,
for they will inherit the whole earth.

Humble in this context actually means *meek*, which is a letdown for people, because they think it means weakness. That's not true.

Meekness is strength used at the appropriate time. It's speaking softly and carrying a big stick, to quote Teddy Roosevelt.

Maybe you don't think that being quiet makes a difference to people, but you're wrong. Meekness speaks louder than shouting any day, and if you truly focus on maintaining a lifestyle of quiet strength, people will notice.

It's often the things you don't say that make the most difference.

What's the point?
Meekness matters to God. It's not the loud confrontational fighters who are going to be successful in the end. It's the quiet ones in the back. You don't have to be a loud-mouthed bully to communicate what you believe.

✅ May 13
Craving an upright lifestyle

CHRIST-FOLLOWERS ARE supposed to be different, but, like everything else in our lives, it starts with attitude.

Matthew 5:6
God blesses those who hunger and thirst for justice,
for they will be satisfied.

That word *justice* there really means *right standing with God*. We are supposed to desire righteousness, but righteousness isn't our default. We're born with an innate desire to do wrong. We have to build healthy habits to seek God and live the way He wants us to. But more than living right, we're supposed to think right too.

This is one of the reasons why it's so important to surround yourself with people who love Christ and follow Him. It's difficult enough to do the right thing in a group of believers; it's so much harder to do the right thing in a group of people who don't understand your worldview. No, don't shut the world out. But if close association with people who don't follow Christ is causing you to stumble, you might want to think about changing your crowd.

What's the point?
Doing the right thing—making wise choices, living the way the Bible says in every area, matters to God—whether it's your thought life or your friendships or marriage or work or church.

The Bible is our guide to right living, and if we do what it says, we'll be content. God doesn't forget and He doesn't ignore. If it feels like a sacrifice to do the right thing, do it anyway because God will make it worthwhile.

✔️ May 14
Mercy enough to share

ATTITUDE ISN'T EASY to hide. It shows in everything you do and in everything you say. People can judge what kind of person you are by how you react. People are always watching your life, but that's hard to remember when someone has made you angry.

Matthew 5:7
God blesses those who are merciful,
for they will be shown mercy.

As Christ-followers, we're supposed to love mercy so much that we look for opportunities to share it. We're supposed to be merciful because we will be shown mercy. And what's more, you'll be happy if you show mercy. Sounds simple enough, right?

Human nature is not so easily thwarted. We're not geared to show mercy. We love to receive it, but showing it is a different story. We need to remember, though, that we've been shown mercy through Christ's sacrifice. For us to withhold mercy from someone else is prideful and selfish and arrogant. Yes, mercy has many forms, but chief among them is love. If you're demonstrating mercy to someone without loving them, it won't make a difference to either of you.

What's the point?
No matter how someone has hurt you, don't strike back. Show mercy. Love them anyway and forgive them. It will be good for you, and it will be good for them, even if it feels like a sacrifice. And if it feels like your sacrifice is going unrewarded, remember what Christ has done for you and remember the future you've been promised.

You have mercy aplenty coming your way. You have enough to share.

✅ May 15

Changing us from the inside out

DO YOU EVER wish that you could see God? I do. It's not that I have a hard time believing in Him. It's just that I would appreciate being able to actually look Him in the eye when I talk to Him. Eye contact means a lot to me, and not being able to see His face is frustrating sometimes.

I would dearly love to be able to see God so I know I'm going the right way, but is there actually a way to see Him?

Matthew 5:8
God blesses those whose hearts are pure,
for they will see God.

In this context, what purity of heart means is having the correct perspective about God, yourself, and your life. When you get that straight on the inside, you'll be able to see God on the outside.

Does it work? Think about it. When you aren't focusing on what God says is right or when your perspective of God is off, He seems far away or silent.

But when you believe what the Bible says about who God is and who you are, then you can see God—not physically, but you can see the results of Him working in your own life and in the lives of others.

What's the point?
When I'm not focused on the things that matter (like loving God and loving people), I'm focused on myself. But when I start taking God at His word, He changes me from the inside out.

God is always working in plain sight, and we just have our eyes closed.

✅ May 18
Peace never just happens

SOMEWHERE PEOPLE GOT the idea that peace will come about just because we are not actively at war with someone. History has proven that conflict is the natural state of the human race. But is peace completely outside our grasp?

Matthew 5:9
God blesses those who work for peace,
for they will be called the children of God.

Human nature precludes peace from being a natural state for us. We're always going to be in conflict with each other unless someone actively makes and maintains peace in the relationship. So if the key to being blessed is to make and maintain peace, how do we do it?

Peace between God and Man came at the price of Jesus' blood, where Jesus accepted the blame for our failures. He did what was right for us, instead of what was right for Him. And I think there's a lesson in that. Conflict comes when someone breaks the law or hurts someone else. Working for peace means making the choice to do what's right.

What's the point?
When it comes to our relationship with God, the only way to make peace is through Christ. But when it comes to our relationships with each other, making and maintaining peace comes down to doing what's right.

Unfortunately, sometimes doing the right thing will cause more trouble between people than it solves. Peace isn't the absence of conflict. Peace is knowing what's right and doing it, in spite of the cost personally.

☑ May 19
Live like a messenger about to get shot

I'M A PEOPLE pleaser, and even thinking about the fact that some people don't like me makes me feel sick inside. But not everyone will like me. Some people will make fun of me simply because of the fact that I follow Christ.

Matthew 5:10-12
God blesses those who are persecuted for doing right, for the Kingdom of Heaven is theirs. God blesses you when people mock you and persecute you and lie about you and say all sorts of evil things against you because you are my followers. Be happy about it! Be very glad! For a great reward awaits you in heaven. And remember, the ancient prophets were persecuted in the same way.

True Christ-followers are shining lights in the darkness. People who don't believe like darkness because they can hide. When a Christian comes along, shining the light of God's truth, that light doesn't let them hide. It reveals their life for what it is, and they are faced with the choice to either turn to Christ or to shoot the proverbial messenger.

It's what happened to Jesus. Why do we think we would be treated differently if we live for Him?

What's the point?
How we live matters to God. Love God. Love people. Do the right thing. Yes.

But we are called to live the kind of life that shines light into the darkest corners of an unbeliever's heart, so that when they see your life, they have only two choices: turn to Christ or turn away from Him.

☑️ May 20

The one thing you have that God wants

CHRISTIANS HAVE BEEN given a precious gift. Salvation is priceless and a relationship with God through Jesus is something we can never earn or buy, but have you ever wondered what you need to do to make God happy?

Matthew 8:5-11
When Jesus returned to Capernaum, a Roman officer came and pleaded with him, "Lord, my young servant lies in bed, paralyzed and in terrible pain."
Jesus said, "I will come and heal him."
But the officer said, "Lord, I am not worthy to have you come into my home. Just say the word from where you are, and my servant will be healed. I know this because I am under the authority of my superior officers, and I have authority over my soldiers. I only need to say, 'Go,' and they go, or 'Come,' and they come. And if I say to my slaves, 'Do this,' they do it."
When Jesus heard this, he was amazed. Turning to those who were following him, he said, "I tell you the truth, I haven't seen faith like this in all Israel!"

Faith matters to God on a level that supersedes anything else. Faith is a powerful thing, and it's the one thing that Jesus pointed out over and over and over again as something God wants.

What's the point?
You have one thing you can give that will please God. Your trust. You can choose to put your faith in God, even when you don't feel like it.

Nothing makes Him happier.

✓ May 21
Living like salt and light is a calling

CHRISTIANS ARE OFTEN called salt and light. I used to wonder what on earth that meant. As I've studied, I understand the concept better now, but one thing I only recently realized is that living a life that is salt and light to other people isn't something we can do by ourselves. It's a calling.

Matthew 5:13-16.
You are the salt of the earth. But what good is salt if it has lost its flavor? Can you make it salty again? It will be thrown out and trampled underfoot as worthless. You are the light of the world—like a city on a hilltop that cannot be hidden. No one lights a lamp and then puts it under a basket. Instead, a lamp is placed on a stand, where it gives light to everyone in the house. In the same way, let your good deeds shine out for all to see, so that everyone will praise your heavenly Father.

An example? I'm called to be a writer, but until God does something through my writing, I'm just scribbling on a page. So while I wait, I prepare and become the best writer I can be, believing that God will use me someday.

What's the point?
We are called to be salt and light, to live differently, but we can't accomplish that kind of lifestyle without putting Christ first in our lives. If we focus on the things that matter to God, our lives will be different naturally.

If you love God, love people, do right, love mercy, walk humbly, and keep believing, your life can't help but look different.

✓ May 22

What good does worrying do?

LIFE IS FULL of responsibilities, and I drive myself crazy worrying about things that can go wrong. But does worrying really help me?

Luke 12:22-32
Then, turning to his disciples, Jesus said, "That is why I tell you not to worry about everyday life—whether you have enough food to eat or enough clothes to wear. For life is more than food, and your body more than clothing. Look at the ravens. They don't plant or harvest or store food in barns, for God feeds them. And you are far more valuable to him than any birds! Can all your worries add a single moment to your life? And if worry can't accomplish a little thing like that, what's the use of worrying over bigger things?

"Look at the lilies and how they grow. They don't work or make their clothing, yet Solomon in all his glory was not dressed as beautifully as they are. And if God cares so wonderfully for flowers that are here today and thrown into the fire tomorrow, he will certainly care for you. Why do you have so little faith?

"And don't be concerned about what to eat and what to drink. Don't worry about such things. These things dominate the thoughts of unbelievers all over the world, but your Father already knows your needs. Seek the Kingdom of God above all else, and he will give you everything you need.

"So don't be afraid, little flock. For it gives your Father great happiness to give you the Kingdom."

What's the point?
Worry isn't something that matters to God.

He is in control. He will work it out. So let it go, and let Him be God.

✓ May 25

Angry thoughts make an angry life

I USED TO watch what I said all the time. I was afraid to even raise my hand to answer questions in Sunday School because I didn't want to get an answer wrong. But as I've gotten older, I've started speaking my mind more often, which can be good and bad.

But whether you speak or not, what you think will affect the way you live.

Matthew 5:21-22
"You have heard that our ancestors were told, 'You must not murder. If you commit murder, you are subject to judgment.' But I say, if you are even angry with someone, you are subject to judgment! If you call someone an idiot, you are in danger of being brought before the court. And if you curse someone, you are in danger of the fires of hell."

The anger this verse is talking about refers to a consistent state of anger or the act of harboring malice against someone. Notice there's no mention of whether or not they deserve your anger. What we need to see is that Jesus isn't talking about doing anything against that person. He's talking about what you think.

Why? Because anger alone isn't necessarily wrong, but you will become what you think about.

What's the point?
Just because you think something without acting on it doesn't mean you're innocent. Jesus says if you think it, you're just as guilty as if you did it. Anger has its place in our lives, but it should never be a lifestyle.

Take steps to control your anger, before it starts controlling you.

May 26

The kind of love only God can give

WHEN SOMEBODY DOES something mean to me, my first inclination is to do something mean back. I tend to hold to the Golden Rule, but there's a part of me that wants to treat other people the way they treat me. I want people to understand that there are consequences for their actions.

Matthew 5:38-41
"You have heard the law that says the punishment must match the injury: 'An eye for an eye, and a tooth for a tooth.' But I say, do not resist an evil person! If someone slaps you on the right cheek, offer the other cheek also. If you are sued in court and your shirt is taken from you, give your coat, too. If a soldier demands that you carry his gear for a mile, carry it two miles."

Jesus said a lot of crazy stuff, but this one really upset people. He's saying here that if someone hurts you, let them. If someone takes advantage of you, give them more than what they would have taken.

Does that mean we let people walk all over us? No, of course not. It means that we make them aware of the fact that we could fight back but that we're choosing not to—in the name of Jesus.

What's the point?
We won't show the world that we're different by how many Bible verses we know. We will show them that we are different when we love them even though they don't love us back.

That kind of love takes a power only God can give.

May 27

Worry never stops tomorrow from coming

WORRY IS A choice, but sometimes I think we make that choice without thinking about it. I don't know why worrying makes us feel like we have control over life, because worrying stems from the fact that we have no control.

Matthew 6:34
"So don't worry about tomorrow, for tomorrow will bring its own worries. Today's trouble is enough for today."

It's easy to worry about tomorrow or the things we don't understand or can't change. But all worrying does is turn you into someone you're not. Worry might make you feel like you're accomplishing something, but whatever is going to happen will happen whether you worry about it or not.

Worrying about something doesn't mean it won't happen. Worrying about something doesn't mean it will. That's tomorrow. And worrying about it doesn't do you or the people around you any good.

What's the point?

God has it under control and He's going to work everything out. It may not work out today. It may not work out tomorrow. It may not work out in a month or a year. But you can believe that it will work out because that's the way God is.

Whatever is happening in your life right now has a purpose, and God will use it for your good and His glory.

✓ May 28
How does love get smarter?

THE SAME KIND of love isn't good for everyone. Did you realize that?

It's not good to love a complete stranger with the same love you have for your best friend. And vice versa. Even between best friends, there are different kinds of love.

Philippians 1:9-10
I pray that your love will overflow more and more, and that you will keep on growing in knowledge and understanding. For I want you to understand what really matters, so that you may live pure and blameless lives until the day of Christ's return.

Love is a process. Love should always be unconditional, sacrificing, and unselfish. But love looks different to different people.

Some people need flowers. Some people need hugs. Some people need to talk. Some people need to be left alone. Even between best friends or lovers or spouses, love has to look different, though the motivation behind it is the same.

What's the point?
Love is a process. It doesn't happen overnight, and the more you get to know someone, the better you understand what they need. Learning how to love people the way they need to be loved is part of building a relationship with others. It's not easy because everyone is different, but loving each other and building relationships with each other is something that really matters.

The more you learn about other people, the less you focus on yourself.

✔ May 29
Slow down!

STRESS MAKES EVERYTHING worse, especially when you're busy. But stressing out over things you can't control is a waste of time, energy and resources.

We shouldn't worry or be anxious, and most of the time we know better. But we do it anyway. What we're supposed to do is hand it over to God.

Isaiah 64:4
For since the world began,
no ear has heard
and no eye has seen a God like you,
who works for those who wait for him!

It's not our job to run around trying to fix our problems. It's our job to wait on God.

God wants to help us. The God who spun Jupiter in orbit, the One who filled up our oceans and invented the idea of seeds and harvest, would want to take His time and His resources and His energy and invest in my life? Wow.

What can our idols do? What can our petty little celebrities do? What can our vaunted politicians scrambling for national power do? What can our religious leaders do? What can you do? What can I do? Nothing compared to Him.

What's the point?
Don't worry. Wait.

And while you're waiting, enjoy life. Be thankful. Slow down.

We weren't designed to rush through life. We are made to enjoy what God has given us. So let's enjoy it and be thankful.

June 2015

RELATIONSHIPS

Do you have friends? What about family? How about a spouse or a coworker or a boss? Everyone has someone in his or her life, whether it's someone you love or someone you hide from. Sometimes those relationships make life worth living. Other times, relationships can make us wish we'd never been born.

The Bible is full of wisdom when it comes to dealing with the people in our lives. We just have to be humble enough to listen.

June 1
Work at living in peace

DRAMA CONFUSES ME. No, not stage drama. Life drama. Life drama is an incredible waste of time, emotional resources, and opportunity. I don't care for it, and I have a hard time feeling compassion for people who thrive on it.

Which camp do you fall into? It's okay to admit it if you tend toward the drama queen side of the coin. In some cases, being dramatic about stuff is helpful. Those personalities can be valuable in many circumstances because they tend to get stuff done. They tend to prod others into action. They tend to be ferocious doers.

Hebrews 12:14
Work at living in peace with everyone, and work at living a holy life, for those who are not holy will not see the Lord.

Both personalities need each other. It's absolutely possible to work together, but it takes effort on both sides. Working together is harder than it sounds. If you've ever been part of a team, you understand what I mean, but no one person is sufficient on his or her own.

What's the point?
If you're dramatic, recognize it and embrace it. Your intense emotions are a gift, but not everyone around you feels with the same intensity you do. If you're not dramatic, realize that your penchant toward the more logical side of life is also a gift. It's just not as loud.

Try to see the best in each other. Learn from each other. They're in your life for a reason, and God won't let them leave until you learn.

June 2

When solitude becomes a security blanket

I'M INDEPENDENT. I don't need much to make it through in life. I'm not really the sort of person who requires socialization or a circle of friends. It's easy for me to be on my own, and by that token, it's easy for me to isolate myself.

But while I like the quietude of this lifestyle choice, sometimes the silence lies and tries to convince me that I'm isolated because I'm alone.

Hebrews 10:23-25
Let us hold tightly without wavering to the hope we affirm, for God can be trusted to keep his promise. Let us think of ways to motivate one another to acts of love and good works. And let us not neglect our meeting together, as some people do, but encourage one another, especially now that the day of his return is drawing near.

It's easy for me to think that I'm okay without sharing life with people. I can function without them, but there's more to life than just functioning. God didn't put me here to just make it through another day. He wants me to thrive. And I can't do that alone.

What's the point?
Don't cut people out of your life. If you were sufficient on your own, God wouldn't have made other people.

God designed us to invest in each other. So don't run away from it. Embrace it. Yes, that means you're taking a risk. Yes, that means you'll have to give up some time alone. But what are you really here for?

June 3

Real friends share joy

I AM BLESSED to have friends who celebrate with me when I succeed, but I have also had friends (at least they called themselves friends) who didn't find my successes all that exciting. That does something to your heart when the person you've chosen to share a part of your life with doesn't get excited when you are.

For me, a friend who doesn't rejoice with me means I'm being overly emotional or silly, because if it's not worth them celebrating, maybe I shouldn't be celebrating either.

Romans 12:14-16
Bless those who persecute you. Don't curse them; pray that God will bless them. Be happy with those who are happy, and weep with those who weep. Live in harmony with each other. Don't be too proud to enjoy the company of ordinary people. And don't think you know it all!

If you have friends in your life who drag you down, change your friends. Friends are there to help us, to support us, to encourage us, to mourn with us when we're sad and to dance for joy with us when we're happy and generally excited about life. Friends who take your joy and treat it like it's not important aren't friends, and they'll bring more trouble to your life than help.

What's the point?

Share your joy with the people who care about you. There's always more than enough to go around. Yes, it's important to share your sorrows with friends too, but there's something about sharing joy that makes you both better.

June 4

A little love goes a long way

NOT EVERYONE WILL like you. Maybe you try to avoid the people who hate you, but you can't run forever. Eventually, you'll have to talk to them. What do you do when you have to interact with people who want to hurt you?

Romans 12:17-21
Never pay back evil with more evil. Do things in such a way that everyone can see you are honorable. Do all that you can to live in peace with everyone. Dear friends, never take revenge. Leave that to the righteous anger of God. For the Scriptures say, "I will take revenge; I will pay them back," says the Lord. Instead, "If your enemies are hungry, feed them. If they are thirsty, give them something to drink. In doing this, you will heap burning coals of shame on their heads." Don't let evil conquer you, but conquer evil by doing good.

This is one of the tenants of the Christian lifestyle that is difficult to keep to. We are never to take revenge, and instead we are to love the people who hurt us. The only way to do it is to ask God for help, because without His love, you'll fail.

What's the point?
Be kind to those who are cruel to you. Thank them for their help when they treat you like dirt. Encourage them when they discourage you. It's not easy, but God will help you do it.

And who knows what might happen? You never know how God can work in someone else's heart. Maybe all it will take is a little love.

June 5

Instructions for facing the end of the world

IF THE WORLD were going to end today, what would your life look like? If you knew that this was your last day on earth, how would your life change from what it is now? How would your perspective on life change?

Well, I hate to be the bearer of bad news (or good news, depending on how you look at it), but the world will end a lot sooner than most people think.

1 Peter 4:7-8
The end of the world is coming soon. Therefore, be earnest and disciplined in your prayers. Most important of all, continue to show deep love for each other, for love covers a multitude of sins.

The Bible is many things, but I like to think of it as an instruction manual for living. And I find it interesting that the two instructions it gives for facing the end of the world are prayer and love. Is that really all you need to face the end? Don't you need a generator? Don't you need a chemical toilet?

The Bible says to pray and to love each other.

What's the point?
We don't have much time left here, and if we want to make it through, we need to have an intense and unfailing love for our brothers and sisters in Christ. It's the kind of love that doesn't just happen. You have to choose it.

If we have Christ in common, we're family. God will help us sort out our differences. Pray and love and let the end of the world come.

June 8

Give friendship a chance

BEING ALONE ISN'T necessarily bad, being lonely is. And being lonely isn't just depressing, it's dangerous. You can get into trouble when you're always alone, and then what happens? Sometimes you can fall into a pit so deep you can't climb out on your own.

Ecclesiastes 4:9-12
Two people are better off than one, for they can help each other succeed. If one person falls, the other can reach out and help. But someone who falls alone is in real trouble. Likewise, two people lying close together can keep each other warm. But how can one be warm alone? A person standing alone can be attacked and defeated, but two can stand back-to-back and conquer. Three are even better, for a triple-braided cord is not easily broken.

Friendship can be tricky. Any time you open your heart to someone else, you're taking a chance, risking that they will turn on you. And that may happen. But you aren't designed to be lonely, and you can't be who you were meant to be without investing in people or allowing others to invest in you.

What's the point?
One of Satan's great lies is that nobody gets you, but the truth is that more people understand you than you know. And you won't know until you give them the chance.

People are people. Nobody's perfect. Everyone screws up. And people will hurt you. Guess what? You will hurt others too.

Extend the same grace you hope to receive in those moments. And give friends a chance.

June 9

Friends make each other better

EVERYONE ENCOUNTERS obstacles, but some people give up and others press on. Why is that? I truly believe one of the most important factors for those people who press forward are their friends. And they don't even have to be close friends. Even an acquaintance can help someone make the decision to keep going when without them they might have given up.

Proverbs 27:17
As iron sharpens iron,
so a friend sharpens a friend.

Friends keep us sharp, and the sharpest friends are the ones who encourage us, even though it may not be fun at the time. The best friends are the ones who never let you give up, who tell you the truth in love, who jump into the trenches with you.

Encouragement isn't just telling people what they want to hear. Encouragement is building others up, giving them courage. And you don't give someone courage by giving them a reason to sit on the bench. Encouragement isn't easy. It's so much easier just to pat someone on the back and let them roll around in their insecurities and their failures and their insufficiencies. But that's not encouragement, and that's not friendship.

What's the point?
A friend who doesn't challenge you, who doesn't encourage you, won't help you much. Real friends make you better.

If you've got those friends, thank God for them. They're priceless. If you don't, don't give up till you find some. You'll be better off with friends like that in your life.

June 10

Is your friendship about you?

I DON'T LIKE depending on other people, and I don't like asking for help. But there are times when I need it. And in those times, I have an arsenal of amazing people who step up to surround me with prayer and words that have to come straight from God.

Romans 12:10
Love each other with genuine affection, and take delight in honoring each other.

Show me a friendship with genuine affection, and I'll show you friends for life. But genuine affection is a concept, and concepts are great, but they aren't good for much until you put them into practice. So what does it mean? It's giving your friend the bigger slice of cake.

Do you need the attention in the friendship? Do you need to be the one who's at the center all the time? Honestly, ask yourself, because if the answer is yes, I'm sorry to be blunt, but you're missing the point of friendship.

What's the point?
God made friends so we wouldn't have to stand alone, so we could be part of a team, so we could be a part of something bigger than we are.

If you have friends, take the time to find out what they need. Ask them how you can help them. Get involved in their lives for more than just what you need. Practice playing second fiddle. Shower them with the attention. And something amazing will happen. Your friendship will get stronger. Your friends will grow, and so will you.

June 11

Fighting never makes it better

WHEN I'M TIRED or stressed out, sometimes my mouth runs away with me. I have a sarcastic streak too, which can be very funny when it isn't being used for the forces of evil.

Proverbs 15:1
A gentle answer deflects anger,
but harsh words make tempers flare.

People don't like fighting. Maybe they like arguing or disagreements, and both of those are part of every healthy relationship, whether you're best friends or married or even family. But from my experience, people don't like a real fight, especially between two people who care about each other.

If the person who started the fight is already that upset, fighting back isn't going to scare them. It's just going to make them angrier. Yes, it's true that some people just want to fight. Some people are just angry as a general rule. But even people who start fights don't really want to fight. There's usually something else causing their problem, and they're either too scared or too insecure to talk about it openly.

What's the point?
Answer cruel words gently. And if that doesn't work, if the person you're talking to doesn't calm down, stop the conversation or leave. If he or she is that upset, nothing you can say will make it better until they calm down on their own.

Fighting won't solve the problem. Fighting only hurts feelings and separates friends, and I don't know about you, but that's not something I ever want to do.

June 12

Ignoring conflict never makes it better

COMMUNICATION IS HARD work, and even if you do it well, you'll still run into times when something goes wrong and somebody gets his or her feelings hurt. And in those instances, you have to make a decision–let it go or face it.

Matthew 5:23-24
So if you are presenting a sacrifice at the altar in the Temple and you suddenly remember that someone has something against you, leave your sacrifice there at the altar. Go and be reconciled to that person. Then come and offer your sacrifice to God.

Most of the time, it's better to just let it go. Otherwise you'll be making the proverbial molehill into a mountain. But sometimes communication problems start out as mountains, and they'll only get bigger if you don't take steps to correct what went wrong and reconcile with everyone involved.

Let's be honest here. It would be so much easier to just finish doing what you're doing before you track down people to smooth out your relationship. Am I right? But that's not what Jesus says to do. If you realize someone has something against you, drop whatever you're doing right now and go make it right.

What's the point?
Don't run away from conflict. Don't be afraid of it either. Conflict is a natural part of living on Earth, and if we treat it right, we can learn from it and grow stronger as individuals, families, friends, and teams.

It's time to clean house, Christians. Be honest with yourselves. Who have you hurt? And are you courageous enough to face that person?

June 15

The world is full of jerks who need grace

I WISH I could tell you I were the epitome of patience and forgiveness. But I'm not. Not even on my best days. Some people just have a gift for finding every button I have, and they seem to thrill at pushing it over and over and over again.

Sometimes I think they do it on purpose. Most of the time, I don't think they even realize that they're doing it.

Colossians 3:13
Make allowance for each other's faults, and forgive anyone who offends you. Remember, the Lord forgave you, so you must forgive others.

We live in a world where people with the best of intentions still end up walking all over other people. People come in all shapes and sizes and moods and shades and flavors, and God made them all that way for a reason. He's got a special plan in mind for every person (whether they accept that plan is up to them), and while we all do need to do our part, just because your personality doesn't mesh with someone else's doesn't make them wrong. And it doesn't make you wrong either.

What's the point?
Everybody needs grace. Not every person who drives you nuts is a jerk. It could be that they are oblivious to how they are bothering you, and in that case, it's in everyone's best interest to talk it out.

If God is good enough and big enough and great enough to give us grace for the things that we have done, don't you think we can give grace to the people around us?

June 16

Why do we give up on people?

IT'S EASY TO complain about people when they can't hear you. Even if you're saying true things, it's a lot easier to say them when there's no danger of being overheard.

But if it's something you can talk about behind closed doors with people who weren't involved, it's something you ought to talk about with the person who started the problem.

James 4:11-12
Don't speak evil against each other, dear brothers and sisters. If you criticize and judge each other, then you are criticizing and judging God's law. But your job is to obey the law, not to judge whether it applies to you. God alone, who gave the law, is the Judge. He alone has the power to save or to destroy. So what right do you have to judge your neighbor?

Some people are impossible because their standards are so high. Others are impossible because their standards are so low. It doesn't mean that one perspective is wrong and one is right. It just means that we all need a little grace.

If the problem isn't yours, talk to the person who's bothering you quietly, respectfully. If they choose to make a show, that's their problem. But you have to give them a chance to make things right before you give up on them.

What's the point?
Give people the benefit of the doubt. Don't be a coward and complain about the situation where they can't hear. Do something about it in love.

Jesus never gives up on us. So why do we think we can give up on people?

June 17

What you miss when misjudge

I ENDED UP next to an old man on a flight from Atlanta to Wichita. He took one look at me and my WSU t-shirt and said: "Oh, you're one of those #$%& Shockers." And then he proceeded to mutter about idiots and morons as I climbed over him to get to my seat.

Honestly, I didn't know what to say or what to think, so I just tried not to do either. I responded politely, buckled myself in, and then plugged my earphones in for the rest of the flight. I didn't want to talk to him.

I fell asleep after my in-flight snack, and when I woke up, we were descending into Wichita. The grumpy old guy had taken care of my trash and put my tray up for me. I didn't get a chance to talk to him before he deplaned, and I still wonder if maybe I had misjudged.

John 7:24
Look beneath the surface so you can judge correctly.

We hear it all the time: Don't judge. Don't judge. Don't judge. Well, guess what, folks? We have to judge. We judge everything all the time. If we didn't, we'd all be making stupid decisions every moment of our lives.

What's the point?

Every situation, every person, every thing in life is more than it appears. There's always more to the story.

But if you make your judgment call based on something superficial, you may miss the point. And you may miss the opportunity to bless someone or to be blessed yourself.

June 18

Why asking is better than demanding

I DON'T LIKE demanding anything, even if it's the right thing.

But what about us Christians? Have you ever had to confront a fellow Christian and demand that he do the right thing because it's the right thing to do?

Philemon 1:8-9
That is why I am boldly asking a favor of you. I could demand it in the name of Christ because it is the right thing for you to do. But because of our love, I prefer simply to ask you. Consider this as a request from me—Paul, an old man and now also a prisoner for the sake of Christ Jesus.

Onesimus was a slave who had run away from his master, Philemon. Philemon was a Christian, and when Paul met Onesimus in prison and led him to Christ, Paul wrote to Philemon asking him to forgive Onesimus.

If anyone could have pulled rank on Philemon, it was Paul. But Paul didn't operate like that. Philemon was his friend and his brother in Christ and instead of simply demanding that Philemon forgive Onesimus, Paul just asked him instead.

What's the point?
There's a major attitude difference between doing something because you've chosen to do it and doing something because you've been told.

In some cases, you have to pull rank and demand what is right. But if you have the opportunity to ask instead of demand, take it. It'll help you grow in your relationships with others, and it'll give people around you a chance to do the right thing for the right reason.

June 19

Praying for people you dislike

IT'S REALLY HARD to hate someone you're praying for. Even if that person is a villain, someone who has hurt you repeatedly, someone you just don't like, if you are genuinely praying for that person, you will have a hard time hating them. If you pray for them, you will love them. It just happens.

So maybe that's our hesitation to pray for people we don't like: we don't want to love them. We don't want to love people who hurt us. We don't want to love people who use us. We don't want to love people who irritate us. But that's not the way we're supposed to live.

1 Timothy 2:1
I urge you, first of all, to pray for all people. Ask God to help them; intercede on their behalf, and give thanks for them.

Prayer was never meant to be a popularity contest. We're supposed to pray for everyone whether we like them or not, whether we know them or not.

Prayer only requires that you love them enough to ask God to help them. Let God sort it out. There's nothing you can do anyway that will change someone's heart.

What's the point?
If you pray for the people you don't like, you'll watch a miracle happen.

Not that God changes the person who bothers you, but that He changes you.

June 22

Peter and Paul

EVERY CHRIST-FOLLOWER knows another Christ-follower who they don't necessarily get along with, and there's nothing wrong with that. God has used all sorts of different people with all sorts of different relationships to accomplish amazing things for Him.

Philippians 2:1-2
Is there any encouragement from belonging to Christ? Any comfort from his love? Any fellowship together in the Spirit? Are your hearts tender and compassionate? Then make me truly happy by agreeing wholeheartedly with each other, loving one another, and working together with one mind and purpose.

Philippians was written by the Apostle Paul, but there's another verse that's almost identical to this. 1 Peter 3:8, written by Peter the Disciple. And there were never two followers of Christ more different from each other.

Peter was a fisherman. Paul was a scholar. Peter was flamboyant, an intense, emotional person. Paul was a thinker. And let's not forget the most obvious disparity in their relationship. Peter led many to Jesus, and, at the start, Paul killed them. Of course, when God got a hold of Paul, his life changed (and so did his name). But even if God forgets our sins, it's hard for the people around us to do the same.

What's the point?
God has made everyone different, and even if we rub each other the wrong way, we can still work together.

I'm sure Peter and Paul may not have been the best of friends, but they were willing to look beyond their differences because they could agree on what mattered.

Can you?

June 23

No surprises the day after the wedding

WHEN A BOY and girl like each other, something strange happens. There are some exceptions, yes, but the majority of the time, both the guy and the girl are totally absorbed with portraying the perfect image of themselves.

Then, when they finally take the next step and get married, the images they've created vanish, leaving them wondering where the person they fell in love with went.

Proverbs 31:30
Charm is deceptive, and beauty does not last;
but a woman who fears the Lord will be greatly praised.

Charm is great, but let's get real, folks. It's a tool we use to advance a relationship. And beauty? Society and culture tells us we need to look a certain way. Where do we get the idea that beauty comes from what we put on our faces? We need to look for something deeper in people than what they look like or even how they act.

What's the point?

Look for someone who loves God and does what He says and wants to live for Him, because those qualities only get stronger as you get older. When all the glamor wears off and you realize that your wife has acne scars and hairy legs and your husband snores and crunches tortilla chips loud enough to wake the dead, your mutual desire to follow God will remain.

Skip the facade. Be real. Then there will be no surprises after you say "I do."

June 24

Be kind because there is no rewind

I'M DATING MYSELF. Anyone remember VHS cassette tapes with the "Be kind. Rewind!" stickers? I'm not sure if anyone even still has VHS players anymore.

Wouldn't that be nice if it worked that way in real life? If you were unkind to someone, you could rewind the day and do it over again right?

Ephesians 4:32
Instead, be kind to each other, tenderhearted, forgiving one another, just as God through Christ has forgiven you.

Jesus forgave us unconditionally. That means there are no limitations on His forgiveness, and, once you ask for it, He never takes it away or brings it up again. We can learn a lesson from that kind of forgiveness. If you say you forgive someone, honestly forgive them and don't keep reminding them of how they wronged you. He also unconditionally forgave us no matter what we have done. It doesn't matter how dark or depraved our sins are, His blood is strong enough to cover all of them.

What's the point?

It's not our job to be someone else's Holy Spirit. It's not our job to make someone else feel guilty for the way they've treated us. It's our job to forgive them and keep loving them.

Be kind to each other. And when someone isn't kind back to you, forgive them and keep being kind until God thwacks them on the head and makes them understand that what they're doing is wrong.

June 25

Love in spite of success

LIFE IS BACKWARD. So many times we think we know everything there is to know, and then we discover that we really know nothing at all. We think anger will solve a problem when we really need to be kind. We think our knowledge will solve an issue when we really need to trust someone else. We think we have reason to mourn when really we have reason to rejoice.

Romans 12:15
Be happy with those who are happy, and weep with those who weep.

If we love each other, we should be happy for each other. We should rejoice when the people we love experience success or see their dreams come true. But so many times, it doesn't happen that way. When someone we love succeeds, we get jealous. We feel envious of our friends who we love because they have found something we haven't yet. Or because they have achieved something we feel they don't deserve, and we get angry because we feel like we do.

If you really love someone, it doesn't matter what happens between you, you will always love them. If you love someone with the kind of love that God has for us, it won't matter if your friend fails or succeeds, you can't love them more or less.

What's the point?
Real love isn't natural, but it's the kind of love we are supposed to have. It's not convenient, and it's not a feeling that just swells within you. It's a choice. And choices aren't easy to make, but once you make them, you have something to stand on.

June 26

Staying sharp

A KNIFE CAN only cut something so many times before it gets dull. Then you need to sharpen it, but you have to sharpen a knife with something that's just as hard as it is. Otherwise, it won't work.

Proverbs 27:17
As iron sharpens iron, so a friend sharpens a friend.

Friendship is just like trying to keep a knife sharp. If you choose a friend who is at a different place in their walk with God than you are and you decide to make that friend the closest one in your arsenal, you're going to struggle. I'm not trying to be snobbish here. This is just a fact.

If you have one knife made out of steel and another knife made out of wood, what's going to happen to the wooden knife? The wooden knife is going to be destroyed, and the steel knife will only get duller.

But what happens when you put a steel knife with a steel knife? They sharpen each other. That's what happens with friends who are walking with God the same way you are.

What's the point?
If you want to maintain a solid biblical walk, get yourself a solid biblical friendship and hold on to it.

There will be times when it's not fun, especially when you need to admit you've done something wrong. But, more often than not, you'll build a relationship with another believer that will last through your lifetime on earth.

June 29

Small problems never stay small

SOME TIME AGO, I noticed one of my tires was low on air, and I almost didn't do anything about it. But I thought I ought to have it checked out anyway. I took it in to the local dealership, and the mechanic told me that a large nail had pierced right through the sidewall.

It cost me $150 to replace the tire, but at least I knew the tire was okay.

Matthew 13:31-32
Here is another illustration Jesus used: "The Kingdom of Heaven is like a mustard seed planted in a field. It is the smallest of all seeds, but it becomes the largest of garden plants; it grows into a tree, and birds come and make nests in its branches."

Seeds are pretty spectacular little things. They're so tiny, but after you plant them and take care of them, they become such big things. Trees or wheat crops that feed millions. The law of sowing and harvesting is incredible!

But similarly, a virus is a spectacular little thing too. Even though it's microscopic, all it has to do is start multiplying, and pretty soon that tiny little annoyance has become something huge and out of control that can do a lot of damage.

What's the point?
Most problems can be fixed while they're still small. No, it's not fun. Fixing problems is never fun, especially when it's your fault. But it's better to suffer a little and fix the problem while you can before it grows beyond your capabilities.

June 30

Not forgiving hurts the people around you

FORGIVENESS IS ONE of those paradoxes we often encounter in the Bible. We convince ourselves that holding bitterness and resentment against someone else is going to hurt them, but it actually hurts us more. It turns us into bitter, resentful people.

But unforgiveness doesn't just affect you. It also affects the people around you.

Proverbs 17:9
Love prospers when a fault is forgiven, but dwelling on it separates close friends.

There is something about being around unforgiving, bitter people that makes you want to rip your hair out. Why would you want to hang out with someone who refuses to forgive?

Forgiveness can be very difficult. It's tempting to hold on to hate and bitterness, but when you forgive someone else for what they did, you become easier to love. Forgiving others makes you humble, and humility is lovable. Arrogance isn't. Refusing to forgive someone demonstrates that you think you're better than they are, when you're not.

What's the point?

All we puny humans are in the same boat. Nobody's perfect, and we all hurt each other. Even if you need to put some distance between you and the person who hurt you, you can still forgive them for what they did. You don't have to restore them to where they were before, but you can forgive them.

Ask God for the strength to forgive the people who hurt you. It'll make life easier, not just for you but for your friends too.

July 2015

WORRY

We live in a world that thrives on worry, stress, and fear. If you aren't experiencing one or all of those on a regular basis, that generally means you aren't working hard enough. All those negative emotions drain us of our power, our energy, and our focus.

The Bible says that we don't have to live under the burden of worry, stress, and fear. We are free to live a life with Him, which means we don't have to worry about anything.

July 1

Trusting God with your plans

HAVE YOU EVER had to move something heavy? So heavy you had to put it on wheels? I once helped a friend move, and it was quite an ordeal to get all of his things into the rented truck. Some of them were really heavy, and we had to use the ramp to get the heaviest things inside. Being able to roll those heavy things into the truck and let them go was a relief.

That's what we're supposed to do with our plans.

Proverbs 16:3
Commit your actions to the Lord,
and your plans will succeed.

The concept this verse is trying to communicate is the idea of rolling our plans on to God. Our plans are often big and exciting, but they're too much for us to carry alone. We're reduced to rolling them around like boulders. We need to roll those dreams and plans on to God and leave them. Whatever they are, we need to give them to God.

What's the point?
My plans and dreams weigh me down sometimes, and that's why I need to give them to God. If we trust Him so completely, God will use our plans to do more than we ever planned to begin with.

Are your plans too much for you today? Roll them up the ramp and leave them with God. Our lives are too short to spend toiling under the heavy weight of self-inflicted deadlines.

Trust God to do what only He can, and move forward with confidence because of who He is.

July 2

Facing unknowns with what I am sure of

LIFE IS FULL of unknowns, and all of those uncertainties can weigh us down if we let them. True, there are a lot of things I know for sure, and I'm thankful for those. But the things I'm not sure about are always floating around in my brain, screaming loudly and trying to distract from the things I know for sure.

Isaiah 46:10
Only I can tell you the future
before it even happens.
Everything I plan will come to pass,
for I do whatever I wish.

Life is full of unknowns, but we can face them using what we know for sure. I may not know what the next stretch of road in my journey will hold, but I do know that God set it out before me. And if God set me on this road, He would have a reason, and He wouldn't send me alone.

I may not know what's at the end of it, but I know He sent me. The eventual end will be happy because God has promised it will be.

What's the point?
God has revealed what we need to know about the future. As for the blank spots, we know Him, so we know what He does is good.

You can answer those questions because you know who God is. You can face those uncertainties because what you know for sure won't change.

July 3

God-confident planning

IT'S IMPORTANT TO keep God in mind when you're making any sort of plans. Maybe I should be super spiritual and say that you shouldn't make any plans without hearing from God first. And that would be ideal. I think we should all try for that. But honestly there are just a lot of times in life when God isn't going to tell you what to do.

James 4:13-16
Look here, you who say, "Today or tomorrow we are going to a certain town and will stay there a year. We will do business there and make a profit." How do you know what your life will be like tomorrow? Your life is like the morning fog—it's here a little while, then it's gone. What you ought to say is, "If the Lord wants us to, we will live and do this or that." Otherwise you are boasting about your own plans, and all such boasting is evil.

Making plans is good, yes, but don't set them in stone without consulting God about them. And even then, don't set them in stone because chances are you still may have to break them out again.

You have to be flexible. You have to be willing to change your plans because what God has planned is better.

What's the point?
Instead of trying to be self-confident, I need to be God-confident. I need to trust Him.

I need to give Him my plans and let Him do what He wants with them. And I need to be flexible enough to stay when He says stay and brave enough to move when He says move.

July 6

Waiting for God to answer

Psalm 40:1-8
I waited patiently for the Lord to help me,
and he turned to me and heard my cry.
He lifted me out of the pit of despair,
out of the mud and the mire.
He set my feet on solid ground
and steadied me as I walked along.
He has given me a new song to sing,
a hymn of praise to our God.
Many will see what he has done and be amazed.
They will put their trust in the Lord.
Oh, the joys of those who trust the Lord,
who have no confidence in the proud
or in those who worship idols.
O Lord my God, you have performed many wonders for us.
Your plans for us are too numerous to list.
You have no equal.
If I tried to recite all your wonderful deeds,
I would never come to the end of them.
You take no delight in sacrifices or offerings.
Now that you have made me listen, I finally understand—
you don't require burnt offerings or sin offerings.
Then I said, "Look, I have come.
As is written about me in the Scriptures:
I take joy in doing your will, my God,
for your instructions are written on my heart."

What's the point?

No matter what's happening in your life or where you are in your walk, God has a plan. And every now and then you'll get to see a glimpse of what it could be, if you're looking for it.

He won't leave you hanging. Even though it may not be the answer you want (especially if it's not the answer you expect), He will answer.

July 7

His voice is in the thunder

I can't see God. Nobody can. So it's easy to forget who He is and how He works in our lives. It's easy to let the worry and stress of our everyday lives overwhelm us, because those are things we can see.

But we should never forget what God is capable of and what He has done for us.

Job 37:1-5
"My heart pounds as I think of this.
It trembles within me.
Listen carefully to the thunder of God's voice
as it rolls from his mouth.
It rolls across the heavens,
and his lightning flashes in every direction.
Then comes the roaring of the thunder—
the tremendous voice of his majesty.
He does not restrain it when he speaks.
God's voice is glorious in the thunder.
We can't even imagine the greatness of his power.

Can you wrap your head around that? Can you really comprehend having a face-to-face relationship with someone as powerful as God? I can't. I can't fathom it.

What's the point?
Life is tough. You've got too much to worry about. You're overwhelmed with things that stress you out. You're afraid of all the things you don't know. Or maybe you're afraid of all the things you do know.

Remember who your God is. Remember that He can get you through any storm.

The next time a thunderstorm rolls through, take a moment and remember that God's voice is in the thunder. And it's glorious.

July 8

X

Facing the floods without stopping

IF YOU'RE WADING through waters deep enough to cover your head or if you're walking in a forest fire, stopping will mean you die. Stopping your forward momentum means you're in trouble. You're supposed to keep moving. You're supposed to keep going. And this is God's promise that you'll make it through to the other side.

Isaiah 43:2
When you go through deep waters,
I will be with you.
When you go through rivers of difficulty,
you will not drown.
When you walk through the fire of oppression,
you will not be burned up;
the flames will not consume you.

When you go–not when you're standing still—through trouble, God is there. Whether you're fording raging rivers or walking on hot coals, God has promised He'll be with you every step of the way. He doesn't promise you won't get wet. He doesn't promise you won't get burned. But He does promise that you won't be overwhelmed.

You just have to keep moving.

What's the point?
God never leaves His people to fight alone. Whatever you do, don't stop. If you stop, you might be overwhelmed. Just keep going. Just keep believing.

If life has left you timid and tired and weary and worn, don't give up. You're not alone. God hasn't left.

Don't turn your back on Him just because you think He's not listening; He is.

July 9

X

Rescue comes in rising waters

IN TIMES OF trouble and difficulty, it can feel like God has left you to fend for yourself. But when you call for Him, God hears you.

No one can say it better than David. David knew just how promptly God's rescue came. No, He didn't always come when David wanted Him, but God always showed up when David needed Him.

And nothing has changed.

Psalm 18:2-3, 16, 28-29
The Lord is my rock, my fortress, and my savior;
my God is my rock, in whom I find protection.
He is my shield, the power that saves me,
and my place of safety.
He is my refuge, my savior,
the one who saves me from violence.
I called on the Lord, who is worthy of praise,
and he saved me from my enemies.

He reached down from heaven and rescued me;
he drew me out of deep waters.

O Lord, you are my lamp.
The Lord lights up my darkness.
In your strength I can crush an army;
with my God I can scale any wall.

What's the point?
When we call for His help, God charges in with thunder and lightning and earthquakes and terror and reaches down to us to pull us out of our distress and our fear.

So don't give up because you're facing something difficult. God is our light in the darkness, and with Him nothing is impossible.

July 10

[X]

Choose to see what God gives you

IN DIFFICULT SEASONS, you can either choose to focus on everything that's going wrong, or you can look for the tiny ray of light that's shining through the clouds. Because it's there.

It may be small, but it exists. And it's there to remind you that all things happen for a reason, especially the things that seem bad.

Psalm 27:3-5
Though a mighty army surrounds me,
my heart will not be afraid.
Even if I am attacked,
I will remain confident.
The one thing I ask of the Lord—
the thing I seek most—
is to live in the house of the Lord all the days of my life,
delighting in the Lord's perfections
and meditating in his Temple.
For he will conceal me there when troubles come;
he will hide me in his sanctuary.
He will place me out of reach on a high rock.

When you're in those trouble-filled times in life when everything is going wrong, do you realize you have a choice? Yes, you can look at your life and see all the problems you have. But you can also look for the things that are going right.

Which choice do you think is going to help you get through the day?

What's the point?
God has a plan. Sure, things may seem bad to you right now, but that doesn't mean God isn't working them out.

Keep your eyes open. Choose to see the opportunities God is giving you rather than the ones you think He's taking away.

July 13

Praising God because of trouble

PRAISING GOD CHANGES your attitude. What's more, praising God because of the difficulties in our lives makes those difficulties easier to bear.

Trouble doesn't last forever. And when you get on the other side of it, most of the time, you'll be grateful for it when you look back.

Psalm 52:9
I will praise you forever, O God,
for what you have done.
I will trust in your good name
in the presence of your faithful people.

When tough times hit me, I need to be thankful for them. Because someday in the future, I'll look back on this time in my life, and I'll be able to see how valuable these difficulties were.

That's not a coincidence. It's God working. It's God taking the terrible things in our lives and using them for good. It's God making something beautiful out of something our enemy intended for evil, and that's something only God can do.

What's the point?
God takes the trouble in our lives and makes it beautiful. He restores. He redeems. But we don't talk about Him that way enough, so the world doesn't know Him that way.

The world doesn't see a Rock; they see a crutch. They don't see a Judge; they see a sledgehammer.

Maybe if we talked more about the God who rescues us when we're in trouble, the world would see Him as their Savior—and not an option.

July 14

[X]

God has enough strength for you

WE WERE NEVER meant to struggle through life on our own, carrying our own burdens, carrying other people's burdens, weary and worn out. We're supposed to give our burdens to Him.

God is meant to be our strength and our salvation when we hit those hard moments in life, when we cross those low valleys where it's too dark to see, and we're too tired to walk any further.

We're not a disappointment when we lean on His strength; that's what He wants.

Isaiah 33:2
But Lord, be merciful to us,
for we have waited for you.
Be our strong arm each day
and our salvation in times of trouble.

How obvious is that? Why do we always forget the obvious things? I forget the obvious and stress over the problems I can't fix. That's my human experience in a nutshell. But that's not the way a Christ-follower is supposed to live. It's not weakness to rely on God's strength and His help; it's what He expects.

What's the point?
Don't be afraid to draw on God's strength. If you can lean on God's strength before your own wears out, you might get through the low points in life without being so exhausted.

You don't need to be weary. You don't need to reach the breaking point. You don't need to hit the bottom before you ask for His help. You can walk into trouble with His strength instead of your own.

July 15

God listens better than we give Him credit

SOMETIMES LIFE GETS to a certain point where you just can't help but think God doesn't listen. You feel like a nail that's being pounded into unforgiving wood by a hammer that does more to bend it than drive it in. And no matter how much you ask for mercy, more trouble keeps coming.

Psalm 138:3-7
As soon as I pray, you answer me;
you encourage me by giving me strength.
Every king in all the earth will thank you, Lord,
for all of them will hear your words.
Yes, they will sing about the Lord's ways,
for the glory of the Lord is very great.
Though the Lord is great, he cares for the humble,
but he keeps his distance from the proud.
Though I am surrounded by troubles,
you will protect me from the anger of my enemies.
You reach out your hand,
and the power of your right hand saves me.

It's easy to trust what you can see and what you feel because those are the things that are obvious. But we can't trust our feelings, and we can't trust our eyes because the things that are real are the things we can't see. And it's not wrong to ask God to show Himself in those moments.

God wants us to look for Him. He wants us to reach out to Him, and He's not so far away that He can't answer.

What's the point?
Keep your eyes and ears open. No, He may not take your problem away, but just knowing He's there, knowing He's listening, and knowing that He will keep His promise is enough to get you through it.

[X]

Do you really want to know the answer?

GOD WANTS US to search for Him. He wants us to reach out in the darkness and find Him, and He always answers. Not always immediately, but He always answers. The trouble is, do you want an answer?

Searching for answers is easy, but hearing an answer that you don't like is a hard pill to swallow if you want life on your own terms.

Psalm 95:7-8
For he is our God.
We are the people he watches over,
the flock under his care.
If only you would listen to his voice today!
The Lord says, "Don't harden your hearts
as Israel did at Meribah,
as they did at Massah in the wilderness.

God isn't hard to find, but His answers may upset you, especially if you want your own way. We don't want to submit to His rules, and we have this idea that if God is good, He'll let us do what we want. But it doesn't work that way.

What's the point?
God doesn't answer us in ways that make us unhappy to deprive us of our fun. He's not trying to squash us or prevent us from living our lives. He's trying to bless us. He's trying to give us a better life than we can ever earn on our own, the kind of life where you have no regrets.

Because if you twist off on your own, believe me, you'll have regrets. And there's nothing more poisonous to a happy life than regrets.

July 17

[X]

The GPS made me do it

I HEARD A story on the radio that tourists in Alaska kept ending up on a clearly marked airport runway, thanks to a malfunctioning GPS system. But the runway was marked with signs and fences, and the people were doing what the GPS said in spite of the fact that it was obviously wrong.

Sometimes I'm like a broken GPS. I get confused, and then I stubbornly insist that I'm right even when the truth of my ignorance is staring me right in the face.

Isaiah 48:17-18
This is what the Lord says—
your Redeemer, the Holy One of Israel:
"I am the Lord your God,
who teaches you what is good for you
and leads you along the paths you should follow.
Oh, that you had listened to my commands!
Then you would have had peace flowing like a gentle river
and righteousness rolling over you like waves in the sea."

None of us can trust our own senses or our own understanding because we don't have all the pieces of the puzzle. We don't know what the big picture is supposed to look like.

So how on Earth can we know which direction we're supposed to go? That's why we have the Bible. That's why God is leading us in the direction He wants us to go, and He expects us to trust Him.

What's the point?
Don't trust your own understanding. Your spirit's GPS is broken. Instead, do what God says is right.

You'll be less frustrated, and you might even learn to enjoy the ride along the way.

July 20

[X]

A life without something to look forward to

ON MY BIRTHDAY, I go to Starbucks and get a pumpkin latte and a pumpkin scone. I look forward to going every year. Well, one year, I got tired of waiting and went before my birthday. And that was perfectly okay... but when October 15 rolled around, my yearly treat wasn't as exciting as it would have been if I had waited.

I've learned that life is a lot more fun to tackle if you have something to look forward to.

Psalm 27:13-14
Yet I am confident I will see the Lord's goodness while I am here in the land of the living. Wait patiently for the Lord. Be brave and courageous. Yes, wait patiently for the Lord.

God didn't design us to forge through life without hope. Everybody needs hope. None of us are strong enough to make it otherwise, and if you've convinced yourself that you can get through life without expecting God to show up, you should read the Bible and see all the promises that God has made us.

The Bible exists to give us hope, to help us realize (and remember) that we have something coming that's better than what we have now.

What's the point?
Have you ever wondered what would have happened to you if you had no hope? I would have given up long ago. But I believe.

Because of who God is, I am confident that I'll see Him work in my life today. So I wait because I have hope.

July 21

Fearless

THE LONGER WE live and the longer we wait for Christ's return, the more trouble we have to face. And after a while it wears us down, and even though our confidence isn't shaken, little fears start creeping in.

Hebrews 10:35-36
So do not throw away this confident trust in the Lord. Remember the great reward it brings you! Patient endurance is what you need now, so that you will continue to do God's will. Then you will receive all that he has promised.

Fearless confidence isn't something that only super Christians can claim. Fearless confidence stems from trusting God completely, and it's something every Christ-follower can access. In the moments when I'm totally focused on God, I'm not afraid of anything.

But fear is tricky. It's stealthy and deceitful. Fear makes us feel like we have power over our lives, and when it comes down to choosing between fear and confidence, many of us choose fear because it gives us something to do. But fear is hollow and empty and useless. Deep inside, we know that there's no comparison between fear and God, but we choose fear anyway because it's something we can control–or at least that's what we think.

What's the point?
Don't throw away your confidence in God because you run into trouble. Don't choose fear over confidence because you can't control what's coming.

You can't control your life anyway. Isn't it better to trust God? After all, He has a history of keeping His promises.

July 22

The difference a puff of smoke can make

I'VE ALWAYS TRIED to appreciate the things I have when I have them, and I've always tried to be mindful of time. Growing up, everyone always told me how fast time goes, and I thought I'd done a pretty good job of paying attention. I tried to make the most of every second. I didn't waste time yearning and wishing to be older but did the best I could at the age I was.

But I don't think you really appreciate how fast life flies until you've lived enough to look back on it.

James 4:14
How do you know what your life will be like tomorrow? Your life is like the morning fog—it's here a little while, then it's gone.

Our lives are nothing in the grand scale of eternity. They're less than nothing. Our lives are nothing but a puff of smoke. But even 10,000 years fades in comparison to eternity.

Deep inside, all of us want to matter, but we are less than insignificant. That's where God comes in, because a life lived for Him is bigger than a fleeting puff of smoke.

What's the point?
A puff of smoke can't make a difference in the world, but a puff of smoke in God's hands can become something more. That's not something you can accomplish on your own.

God takes what is insignificant and uses it to do great big things–like helping other people generations and generations after our time is gone.

July 23

Overcoming fear

LIFE IS FULL of scary things, and if you focus on all there is to be afraid of, it's easy to be overwhelmed with how little we actually have control over.

Deuteronomy 31:4-8
"The Lord will destroy the nations living in the land, just as he destroyed Sihon and Og, the kings of the Amorites. The Lord will hand over to you the people who live there, and you must deal with them as I have commanded you. So be strong and courageous! Do not be afraid and do not panic before them. For the Lord your God will personally go ahead of you. He will neither fail you nor abandon you."

Then Moses called for Joshua, and as all Israel watched, he said to him, "Be strong and courageous! For you will lead these people into the land that the Lord swore to their ancestors he would give them. You are the one who will divide it among them as their grants of land. Do not be afraid or discouraged, for the Lord will personally go ahead of you. He will be with you; he will neither fail you nor abandon you."

Put yourself in Joshua's shoes. This isn't like a promotion at work. This is like your boss pulling you from a job where you're confident and tossing you into the role of CEO. In mere seconds, you go from being the one who takes orders to the one who gives orders.

What's the point?
Fear can take over your life if you let it, but God wants us to know that He's not going anywhere. The same God who went ahead of Joshua, is the same God who is going ahead of us today.

God knows what the future has in store for us, and He won't let us face it alone. Fear isn't something that you need to give in to because God has given us the power to overcome it.

July 24

Making life make sense

THE BIBLE IS our road map, our instruction manual, and our life coach. It answers our questions, gives us insight into who God is, and reminds us what this life is actually all about. And if you want to know how to stay focused on living the right kind of life, knowing the Bible is essential.

Romans 15:4
Such things were written in the Scriptures long ago to teach us. And the Scriptures give us hope and encouragement as we wait patiently for God's promises to be fulfilled.

On almost every page, God makes a promise or refers back to a promise He already made that He will keep. Because the Bible reveals who God is, we can trust that God will keep those promises.

When life gets crazy, it's easy to lose focus and just look out for yourself. It's easier to just watch your own back. But God doesn't allow anything into our lives without reason, and He doesn't expect us to face difficult times alone either. He's right there with us, and all we have to do is ask for His help. That's what the Bible says. That's what God has promised.

What's the point?
Read the Bible with purpose. Read the Bible with expectation. Search the Internet for verses on certain topics and then instead of just reading the one verse, read the whole chapter. And when you start reading, tell God what you're looking for. Whether you're looking for an answer or just encouragement, I promise you'll find it.

Don't try to make sense of life without it.

July 27

Directions from an outdated map

HAVE YOU EVER tried to give directions from an outdated map? That's a foreign concept to most people now because of digital navigation services, but there was a time when you had to rely only on paper maps. And if your paper map was wrong, you were going to be in a heap of trouble.

Asking for life directions is similar, but God has told us everything we need to know about how to get where we're going. The beautiful thing about the Bible is that it's never outdated.

Isaiah 48:17
This is what the Lord says—
your Redeemer, the Holy One of Israel:
"I am the Lord your God,
who teaches you what is good for you
and leads you along the paths you should follow.

We're born lost. You can follow your own rules, follow your own directions, follow your heart or whatever you want to call it from dawn until dusk, but you'll end up going in circles because the core of who we are inside is lost.

Some choices aren't clear cut. Sometimes you have two good choices. But more often than not, you have a right choice and a wrong choice, and if you've listened to the Bible, you'll know the difference. But choosing the right over the wrong isn't always easy. It's better, but it's not easy.

What's the point?
The Bible never needs updating, and you can always trust it. God gave us the Bible so that we wouldn't be lost.

But it's up to us to follow the directions.

July 28

God has you covered

PART OF HAVING faith is acting like you believe even if you don't feel like it. If you think about it, that's a definition of faith. And the rest of it is remembering.

Isaiah 26:4
Trust in the Lord always,
for the Lord God is the eternal Rock.

Does worry mean I don't trust God? That's what I'm concerned about. Because I want to trust Him completely. I want to know that I've given everything I have over to Him and that He can do whatever He likes with it. Granted, He can do whatever He likes with it without my permission or not, but my attitude about His sovereignty in my life is essential.

The key to facing worry down is remembering who is in charge. If what you are worrying about happens, God has you covered and has something for you to learn.

If what you are worrying about doesn't happen, God still has you covered and has something for you to learn. Either way, God still has you covered.

What's the point?
Giving in to worry is a waste of time, and losing sleep over something you can't change is silly. It's one thing to want to be prepared to face trouble. That's wisdom. But get prepared and then don't worry about it.

When your brain starts to worry anyway, point out to yourself all the ways that God has helped you personally in the past. You'll probably have to remind yourself more than once.

July 29

[X]

How TSA reminded me not to worry

THE LAST TIME I was in the Seattle airport, I ran into a security line of epic length. I just knew I would miss my flight. I started stressing out, but then the Holy Spirit punched me in the head and reminded me to pray.

So I did.

Just then, the security dude waved me into a different line—where I didn't have to take off my shoes, my belt, my jacket, or my hat. And I got to throw everything on the belt and walk through the scanner.

I got through security in 12 minutes. I made it to my gate with time to spare. And I sat there sipping coffee and kicking myself.

Philippians 4:6
Don't worry about anything; instead, pray about everything. Tell God what you need, and thank him for all he has done.

There are so many things in my life that I want to worry about. There are so many things in my life that I want to control. There are so many things in my life that I think I need to fix. The plain and simple truth is that I'm powerless to really do anything at all about these things, and I need to fully rely on God for every step I take, every breath I breathe.

What's the point?
Next time you need something, ask God for it. Don't worry about it. Tell God about it and let Him handle it.

It's easier to say it than to do it, but whenever He works something out, the results are a lot better than when we try to go our own way.

July 30

[X]

Let the toaster do its job

I WATCHED A man hovering over a toaster in a hotel breakfast room today. Maybe he was afraid his toast would burn (understandable), but his actions made me think he was less worried about burning it and more convinced that his hovering would make it toast faster.

Exodus 14:13-14
But Moses told the people, "Don't be afraid. Just stand still and watch the Lord rescue you today. The Egyptians you see today will never be seen again. The Lord himself will fight for you. Just stay calm."

Moses said this to the Children of Israel just before God parted the Red Sea to escape Pharaoh's army. There was no way they could have survived on their own, so God had to intervene. And there was nothing any of them could have done about it. They just had to sit back and wait.

Sometimes we have to wait, and the more we stick our noses where they don't belong, the more trouble we'll make for ourselves before God does what He was going to do all along.

The guy who wouldn't leave the toaster alone should have just let the toaster do its job. Even with all his fussing, he ended up with burned toast.

What's the point?
Are difficulties rushing at you in a tidal wave bigger than you think you can survive? God hasn't left you, and He won't. Just trust Him. He'll step in and save the day, just like He has done throughout history. But He'll do it in His own time and in His own way.

Be still. He's God. He's got it handled, and He doesn't need our help.

July 31

Opinions can be a trap

YOU CAN'T LIVE your life based on other people's opinions. Well, maybe you can, but it's not healthy or productive. People's opinions change and oftentimes they are based on untruths or bias.. It's good to seek opinions, but it's rarely wise to build your life on them.

Proverbs 29:25
Fearing people is a dangerous trap,
but trusting the Lord means safety.

Be careful of other people's opinions. Opinions are good, and it's good to voice your opinions if they're constructive and humble and well-intentioned, but if you're going to voice your opinion, recognize that your word isn't gospel. People have a right to disagree with you, and just because they disagree doesn't mean they hate you. That's part of the problem in America right now. We have this idea that disagreeing with someone equals hate or dislike, and that's not true. Disagreement is one of the things that made this country. Disagreement is healthy. No one who is honest will believe that everyone will agree on every topic.

So be free to voice your opinions, but be okay if people disagree with you.

What's the point?
Getting the opinion of a trusted friend is a good idea. Always. If it's someone you know is grounded in truth, someone you know is dedicated to doing what God says is right, you can probably trust their opinion because they trusted God first.

But when the clock of the universe stops ticking, the person who will be responsible for your choices in life is you.

August 2015

LIVING SPIRIT-LED

Just as worry and stress and fear will drain you of your focus, living a Spirit-led life will energize you. But what is a Spirit-led life? Saying it sounds creepy or uber-religious, but there's nothing creepy or religious about it.

When you accept Christ as your Savior, the Holy Spirit, God Himself, comes to live inside you. He becomes your connection to God the Father. The Holy Spirit is always with us, our constant companion, our comforter and advisor, but most of the time we ignore Him because we don't understand Him.

It is absolutely possible to accept Christ as your Savior but refuse to live a life that is led by the Holy Spirit. But we're not called to that kind of life. We're called to walk through life with the Holy Spirit at our side. So why wouldn't we listen to Him?

August 3

Choosing to live by the Spirit

I HAVE AN orchard here at my little farm. It's nothing spectacular, just a few apricot trees and pear trees that give new definition to the concept of organic.

But in springtime, after the blossoms have fallen, the fruit starts to appear. And it's a good reminder for me that trees that don't look like they're accomplishing anything are actually working–they're producing fruit.

Galatians 5:16-18
So I say, let the Holy Spirit guide your lives. Then you won't be doing what your sinful nature craves. The sinful nature wants to do evil, which is just the opposite of what the Spirit wants. And the Spirit gives us desires that are the opposite of what the sinful nature desires.

These two forces are constantly fighting each other, so you are not free to carry out your good intentions. But when you are directed by the Spirit, you are not under obligation to the law of Moses.

You can believe in Christ but not allow the Spirit to work. So what is Spirit-led living? It's balance. You aren't ruled by emotion. You aren't ruled by the law. You're ruled by the Spirit. Living by the Spirit means you have to know what God wants, you have to talk to God, and then listen.

What's the point?
Make up your mind. You can be a Christian and cling to your hell insurance, or you can choose to let the Spirit lead.

It's not required to live by the Spirit if you're a Christ-follower, but it's the kind of life that God desires for us.

August 4

Living a world-changing love

AMERICAN ENGLISH is a melting pot that gets bigger and lazier every year, yet we still have only one word for *love*. Other languages have multiple words for different kinds of love. Like Greek. Greek has a ton of them.

If you've been around the church you may have heard the term *agape*, which is one Greek word for *love*. *Agape* love is the kind of love that only can be produced by having God's Spirit in our lives, and there happens to be a whole chapter on this kind of love in the Bible.

1 Corinthians 13:4-7
Love is patient and kind. Love is not jealous or boastful or proud or rude. It does not demand its own way. It is not irritable, and it keeps no record of being wronged. It does not rejoice about injustice but rejoices whenever the truth wins out. Love never gives up, never loses faith, is always hopeful, and endures through every circumstance.

It's hard enough to have this kind of love for the people we like, let alone the people we can't stand. But this kind of love doesn't come naturally to anyone, and that's why we need God's help.

What's the point?
God can help us love people we don't even like. It doesn't have to be a huge display. More often than not, love is in the small things—a smile, a hug, holding a door, a kind word, a listening ear.

None of those are world shattering, but they just might be world changing.

August 5

Loving those who hate you back

I LOVE THE way Jesus teaches because He was (and is) a storyteller. That's one of the reasons why I'm wild about stories, because they do more than just entertain. Stories teach.

People came from everywhere to hear Jesus tell stories, and His stories challenged everything they believed.

Luke 10:33-35
Then a despised Samaritan came along, and when he saw the man, he felt compassion for him. Going over to him, the Samaritan soothed his wounds with olive oil and wine and bandaged them. Then he put the man on his own donkey and took him to an inn, where he took care of him. The next day he handed the innkeeper two silver coins, telling him, "Take care of this man. If his bill runs higher than this, I'll pay you the next time I'm here."

The Parable of the Good Samaritan is one of the best known of Jesus' stories. Samaritans weren't Jewish. They were a mixed race people, and the Jews despised them. Generally speaking, Samaritans were bad. So I'm sure when listeners heard Jesus say a Samaritan was coming, they thought he would finish the poor victim off. But he didn't.

What's the point?
Even if people hurt you or hate you, Christ-followers are called to love in return.

It's a difficult choice to love someone who hates you, and it won't make sense to many others. But living Spirit-led means that you love people who don't deserve it.

August 6

Responding to brokenness with joy

OUR WORLD IS a pretty sad place. Everything's broken, and brokenness is always sad. But I have met people who have every right to be unhappy, yet somehow they are more cheerful than people who have everything.

If you're a Christ-follower, you have the Holy Spirit inside you. That means you can access God's power at any time. That's how you can make it through a day or a week or a month or a year with a cheerful heart.

Galatians 5:22-23
But the Holy Spirit produces this kind of fruit in our lives: love, joy, peace, patience, kindness, goodness, faithfulness, gentleness, and self-control. There is no law against these things!

You'll see this passage pop up a few more times in this chapter, because this is the defining list about the qualities a Christ-follower should have in his or her life.

The Bible uses the same word for joy as it does for happiness. The difference comes in where your joy/happiness comes from. It should never depend on your circumstances. Instead, it should be a response to whatever God is doing in your life.

What's the point?
You have the power to choose joy. Whatever the situation, if you have the Holy Spirit in your life, you can choose to respond to your circumstances with joy. Once you choose to respond with joy, even if everything is broken, life looks different.

So smile. The world may be broken, but if you belong to Christ, you're not.

August 7

Peace always costs something

EVERYONE WORRIES. The only real way to deal with anxiety is to live by the Holy Spirit, because one of the fruit (or the results) of living by the Holy Spirit is peace.

You can't buy this kind of peace. You can't earn it either. This kind of peace is something God produces in our lives when we live by the Holy Spirit.

John 14:27
I am leaving you with a gift—peace of mind and heart. And the peace I give is a gift the world cannot give. So don't be troubled or afraid.

According to Jesus, the world does offer a kind of peace. But it's temporary. The world's peace is something you buy, something you control, something you turn on and off. It's not based in anything but emotion, and it's not strong enough to stand up under real pressure.

God's peace depends on God. It cost Him the life of His Son, but He gives it to us free of charge. It's not something that can be taken away, and it never runs out no matter how many times you draw on it.

What's the point?
Whatever you're facing today, if you have God's Spirit, you have God's peace. Worry is a choice. Like joy, it's a response to circumstances, and you can choose peace. God already paid for it. Everyone who follows Him has access to it.

It'll do wonders for your attitude, for your perspective, and your hair color.

August 10

Fix your thoughts

SO MUCH OF our lives revolves around our focus. We do what we focus on. We are what we think. That's why it's so important to have a healthy thought life because what you think is eventually how you will live.

God's peace is a gift, but He doesn't just offer emotional peace. He offers intellectual peace as well.

Isaiah 26:3
You will keep in perfect peace
all who trust in you,
all whose thoughts are fixed on you!

Peace of mind, peace in our thoughts, is something that everyone searches for. Peace of mind eludes us so many times because our thoughts are fixed on things they shouldn't be. We worry because we think about things that don't matter. We're upset or frightened or disturbed because we're focusing on ourselves or on our circumstances, and we're not supposed to focus on those things. We're supposed to focus on God and commit ourselves to Him and lean on him and hope confidently in Him.

What's the point?
Peace is a gift. God has given peace to every one of His followers, and it's our choice to use it. God has given us the power to choose what we think about, and if we focus our thoughts on Him and what He's doing and who He is, peace will follow.

Fix your thoughts on who God is today. Remind yourself exactly who your heavenly Father is, and then look at your circumstances. And I bet your perspective might change a little.

August 11

You may not be able to trust what you feel

I LOVE MY emotions. I wouldn't want to go through life without them, and they help me connect to God on many levels where just plain knowledge falls short. God created us with emotions for a reason, and our emotions can be used to bring Him glory. But my emotions don't always work the way they're supposed to, so I can't always trust them.

Emotions are just like every other part of life. If they don't match up with what is in the Bible, they're going to make trouble for you.

Romans 5:1-2
Therefore, since we have been made right in God's sight by faith, we have peace with God because of what Jesus Christ our Lord has done for us. Because of our faith, Christ has brought us into this place of undeserved privilege where we now stand, and we confidently and joyfully look forward to sharing God's glory.

The first step to peace of heart is to know who God is, through prayer and Bible study and daily worship. The next step is to trust Him. And that's not something anyone else can do for you. That's between you and God. But the longer you know Him, the easier it is to trust Him; and the more you trust Him, the more peace you'll have.

What's the point?
You can't always trust what you feel. First, trust what you know.

Check your heart. Align with God. And pray. And peace will come.

August 12

Good things come to those who wait

PATIENCE IS A characteristic that we grow over time. We don't just wake up with it. That would be nice, but it's one of those qualities we have to develop.

But patience is more than a character quality. It's a gift.

Galatians 5:22-23
But the Holy Spirit produces this kind of fruit in our lives: love, joy, peace, patience, kindness, goodness, faithfulness, gentleness, and self-control. There is no law against these things!

Patience is a gift that God gives us when we accept Christ. It's our choice to use it or not. If you ignore it, you're going to walk into a lot of situations where you aren't prepared and you'll probably end up falling on your face. But if you implement it, you'll always be ready for the challenges that are coming.

Well–maybe you won't be ready, but you'll be as prepared as you can be. And by the time the challenge gets to you, you'll already have lots of practice waiting on God, and that's the best way to prepare for any circumstance.

What's the point?
If you're faced with a choice today — to do or to wait — you might think about waiting. Granted, if you've been waiting and waiting and waiting, double check. Make sure waiting is what God wants. But if you're getting ready to run off half-cocked to do things your own way, you might think twice.

Waiting for God is always better than running ahead of Him.

August 13

Our struggles have a greater purpose

HOW MANY TIMES do we look at the circumstances in our lives as punishment from God? Sometimes they might be. If you've made foolish choices, you may just be facing the consequences. But many times Christ-followers have to face difficulties just because God has a bigger plan.

John 9:1-3
As Jesus was walking along, he saw a man who had been blind from birth. "Rabbi," his disciples asked him, "why was this man born blind? Was it because of his own sins or his parents' sins?" "It was not because of his sins or his parents' sins," Jesus answered. "This happened so the power of God could be seen in him."

This is an old Sunday School favorite, and usually everyone focuses on how Jesus healed the guy. And that's great and important. But what I think is also important is that this man was born blind **so the power of God could be seen in Him**. He was born blind just so Jesus could heal him at that moment.

How patient did this man have to be all those years? To sit and wait and beg until Jesus came? If you think of it this way, we know very little of suffering in 21st Century America.

What's the point?
Whatever you're struggling with today, be patient. You aren't suffering for no reason, and the challenges you're enduring present you with an opportunity to display God's glory for everyone to see.

Who knows? Maybe in 2,000 more years, someone will hear about you and find a reason to be patient when they didn't have one before.

August 14

Being patient with other people

DO YOU EVER just want to smack someone? I do, but instead I usually take notes about them to use them in my next novel (you've heard it's not wise to upset a writer, haven't you?). But is that the way we're supposed to be?

Colossians 3:13
Make allowance for each other's faults, and forgive anyone who offends you. Remember, the Lord forgave you, so you must forgive others.

I'm not very good at making allowances for the faults of others. I think it's my own perfectionism. Deep down inside, I hold myself to such high standards that I expect others to perform at a certain level, and if they don't, I get impatient with them. After all, excellence isn't that hard to achieve. If I can do it, why can't they? Right? Any other perfectionists out there hear me?

But the heart of today's verse is patience and humility. Maybe I'm driven to be perfect, but I guarantee you that I'm not. No one is. And everybody knows that, but there's a difference between knowing it and living it.

What's the point?
When someone wrongs you, forgive them. Because it won't be very long before you turn around and wrong someone else, whether you intend to or not. And you appreciate being forgiven, don't you? You appreciate people being patient with you, don't you?

God forgave us. And when God forgives, He puts our faults out of His mind. They don't exist to Him anymore. And that's how we need to forgive others.

August 17

You can be kind and good

I WANT TO be the sort of Christ follower who everyone knows is different but not at the expense of how I treat people. I know Christ followers who are unkind. I'm sure everyone does. But, boy, are they are good Christians! Those Christians have Bible knowledge that would take me a lifetime to obtain, but are they known for their kindness?

What matters more?

Galatians 5:22-23
But the Holy Spirit produces this kind of fruit in our lives: love, joy, peace, patience, kindness, goodness, faithfulness, gentleness, and self-control. There is no law against these things!

Kindness is a gift of the Holy Spirit, but the word in Galatians actually translates as both kind and good. This is the kindness that sees and understands that people aren't perfect and chooses to be nice to them anyway. This is the kindness that God shows us because He is 100% good, and even though we don't deserve it, He does it anyway.

That's the sort of kindness we need in our lives, and that's what the Holy Spirit will produce if we allow Him to.

What's the point?
Ask the Holy Spirit to show you how to be kind, and He will give you the strength.

Our world glorifies cruelty, both overt and passive, and it's tempting to think that we must be cruel in return if we want to survive. But living a Spirit-led life means that we should be kind, and God says we can stand for what is right without being cruel.

August 18

Kindness that meets real needs

KINDNESS IS MORE than just feeling love or compassion for someone else. Kindness is action, like love. If you see a real need, take steps to meet it, but make sure you meet that need the way God would do it.

Colossians 3:12
Since God chose you to be the holy people he loves, you must clothe yourselves with tenderhearted mercy, kindness, humility, gentleness, and patience.

English doesn't have a word that encapsulates the concept of being both kind and good. The word for kindness here, which is the same word used in describing the Fruit of the Spirit, actually means *useful kindness*. It's helping people according to God's will and timing. I had always assumed that kindness just meant being nice to people.

Spirit-led kindness is helping people the way God does, dealing with the real heart problems instead of the outside issues. We don't always know how to help someone until God shows us, but He will always equip us to help someone else in His name. If He doesn't, maybe you're not the one who needs to barge in with your two cents.

What's the point?
When you're trying to help someone, don't focus on the outside. We try to control behavior instead of fixing the heart, and that's where the problem is. Our hearts need to be healed, and God is the only one who can do that.

The best way to help someone is to meet their real needs and point them to Christ.

August 19

Being good enough

DEEP DOWN, I believe that everybody wants to be good, but goodness doesn't come from us. We don't know how to be good. Goodness is something the Holy Spirit produces in our lives when we accept Christ.

Galatians 5:22-23
But the Holy Spirit produces this kind of fruit in our lives: love, joy, peace, patience, kindness, goodness, faithfulness, gentleness, and self-control. There is no law against these things!

The word *goodness* here actually means *benevolence*, which is the heart that yearns to help others even when there's nothing in it for us. It is the kind of goodness that God will produce in our lives if we let Him. We're not born with the desire to sacrifice. We're not born with the urge to help other people. We're not born good.

God knows that. He doesn't expect us to be good enough. He expects us to look to Him and trust Him, and He will count our faith in Him as being good enough. And the more we look to Him, the more we trust Him, the more we get to know Him, the more goodness will grow in our lives.

What's the point?
You're surrounded by people who need help, but if you lack the strength to help them, ask God for it. He'll provide.

And when you get the chance to help someone else, make sure you help them understand why you're helping. Yes, you love them, but more than that—God loved them first.

August 20

Do good because you believe

BEING GOOD IS an admirable goal that no one can achieve. Doing good is much easier, but I'm not good enough to do good simply because I *am* good.

If I have the Holy Spirit in my life, I'll do what's right because I have faith in who Jesus is.

James 2:14-17
What good is it, dear brothers and sisters, if you say you have faith but don't show it by your actions? Can that kind of faith save anyone? Suppose you see a brother or sister who has no food or clothing, and you say, "Good-bye and have a good day; stay warm and eat well"—but then you don't give that person any food or clothing. What good does that do? So you see, faith by itself isn't enough. Unless it produces good deeds, it is dead and useless.

It's good to do good deeds because it's the right thing to do, but with that kind of thinking, how long will you keep doing good deeds? Because if I'm just doing good deeds for the sake of doing them, I'm going to get tired. But if I'm doing good deeds for others because God has said it's right, that becomes evidence of my faith.

What's the point?
Choose to do good deeds for others because you believe in Christ, not because you are a good person.

Living a Spirit-led life will be full of goodness, but it's not your goodness. It's God's.

August 21

What is faith and how do we find it

I DON'T THINK of faith as a spiritual gift often, but it is. Once you choose to believe in Jesus, the Holy Spirit gives you faith. But faith goes beyond the fuzzy, ethereal, feel-good pep talks some Christians use when they feel like waxing eloquent about something. Faith is a choice, and if you are a follower of Christ, faith is something God has already given you.

Galatians 5:22-23
But the Holy Spirit produces this kind of fruit in our lives: love, joy, peace, patience, kindness, goodness, faithfulness, gentleness, and self-control. There is no law against these things!

Faith is consulting the Bible before you check with your favorite talk show host. Faith is talking to God about a situation before you call a Christian radio station. Faith is letting go of what you know you don't need to hold onto, even though your peers look at you like you've lost your mind. Faith is seeing Him in small things, in big things, in everything.

We have to make the choice to take God at His Word, and once you do that, the Bible won't seem so far out anymore. You'll stop looking at coincidences and start seeing purpose and plan. And the more you get to know Jesus, the easier it is to let Him take over your life.

What's the point?
Faith is the still, small voice at the bottom of your heart urging you to take a chance on God.

Heroes of faith through history weren't special. They were just people who listened and obeyed.

August 24

Let God drive

I DON'T TURN over control of my car to just anyone. It has to be someone whose driving I trust, though even then it's still difficult for me. My brother, for example, is a great driver. So I let him drive us to Dallas a while back because he knew how to get there.

He knew how to drive my car. He knew the roads, the exits, the area. He knew where not to go. He knew how fast he could go. He knew all the specifics, and he knew them in the dark. I didn't know all those things.

Maybe I could have eventually gotten there, but it would have taken longer. How many of us are willing to do that with our lives?

Psalm 9:10
Those who know your name trust in you,
for you, O Lord, do not abandon those who search for you.

Do you trust God enough to turn your life over to Him? That's faith on a different level than just believing Jesus paid for your sins. That's giving your life, your future, your destiny to God completely.

What's the point?
You can try to find your own way through life without God, but you're going to take wrong turns. You'll get lost. You'll run into trouble. Wouldn't it be so much better to just let God drive?

It won't be easy, especially if you like to be in control. But if you trust the one driving, all you'll need to do is relax and hold on for the ride.

August 25

Humble calm that can still bash skulls

SOMEWHERE CHRISTIANS got the idea that gentleness means we don't get to stand up for what's right. We embrace this concept of Jesus as a soft-spoken pansy who never challenged anyone. If you believe that, you should read the Gospels. Jesus challenged everyone and everything, but He did it right.

Matthew 21:12-13
Jesus entered the Temple and began to drive out all the people buying and selling animals for sacrifice. He knocked over the tables of the money changers and the chairs of those selling doves. He said to them, "The Scriptures declare, 'My Temple will be called a house of prayer,' but you have turned it into a den of thieves!"

Jesus got mad, but notice how He handled His anger. He didn't lose control. He simply righted the problem, and He backed up His actions with Scripture.

One of the gifts of the Holy Spirit is gentleness, or meekness, which basically means quiet strength. It's inner calm and humility that doesn't hesitate to bash skulls when needed.

Jesus is the Lamb of God and the Lion of Judah. A paradox? No. That's meekness. And if you can live that way too, that's evidence of God working in your life.

What's the point?
There's nothing wrong with speaking out, but when we're angry, we need to ask for meekness.

It's the balance between standing up for what's right and speaking truth in love. That kind of understanding comes from God.

August 26

True mastery from within

ESTABLISHING GOOD, healthy habits is a great idea, but when it comes down to mastering ourselves, it takes a power stronger than we are to do it.

If you read the Bible, you'll discover that true self mastery doesn't come from something that you do; it comes from the inside when we have the Holy Spirit.

Galatians 5:22-23
But the Holy Spirit produces this kind of fruit in our lives: love, joy, peace, patience, kindness, goodness, faithfulness, gentleness, and self-control. There is no law against these things!

The word *self-control* in this verse is sometimes translated as *temperance*. Anyone who's heard of temperance probably associates it with not drinking alcohol, but in this context the word means "true mastery from within" and can only be achieved by the Holy Spirit.

Spirit-led temperance is not overly focusing on one area of your life. It's letting God into all of them. It's doing what Jesus would do in every situation, not just the ones you want to get His advice on, from "Would Jesus help that little old lady carry her groceries?" to "Would Jesus eat a second bowl of ice cream?"

What's the point?
Stop reading the 12-step books or following the latest fad diets. The best way to control yourself is to get to know Jesus better. Ask Him what He would do for the big decisions and the small decisions.

Don't hold anything back because you think He won't care. Living Spirit-led is about giving God control over every area of your life, even the details.

August 27

You can only walk one road

LIFE COMES DOWN to two options, we either follow Jesus or we do what we want. And as long as you choose to follow your own path, you are subject to the Law, which means you have to pay for your own sins.

Galatians 5:19-23
When you follow the desires of your sinful nature, the results are very clear: sexual immorality, impurity, lustful pleasures, idolatry, sorcery, hostility, quarreling, jealousy, outbursts of anger, selfish ambition, dissension, division, envy, drunkenness, wild parties, and other sins like these. Let me tell you again, as I have before, that anyone living that sort of life will not inherit the Kingdom of God. But the Holy Spirit produces this kind of fruit in our lives: love, joy, peace, patience, kindness, goodness, faithfulness, gentleness, and self-control. There is no law against these things!

If you live life on your own terms, your world will be full of things that can destroy you if you take them to extremes. But if you choose to live Spirit-led, your world will overflow with things you can't get too much of.

You can't have too much love or too much joy. You can't have too much goodness or gentleness or meekness or kindness. None of the Fruit of the Spirit taken to extremes will hurt your life.

What's the point?
If you're not following Christ, you're following yourself. You can't have it both ways.

So make up your mind, because you can't walk two roads at the same time.

August 28

Singing in the dark

IF YOU'RE LIVING Spirit-led, joy will be evident in every aspect of who you are, whether you are an American Christian who suffers in the court of popular opinion, or if you're a Christian in other parts of the world who faces real physical danger for your faith.

Acts 16:22-26
A mob quickly formed against Paul and Silas, and the city officials ordered them stripped and beaten with wooden rods. They were severely beaten, and then they were thrown into prison. The jailer was ordered to make sure they didn't escape. So the jailer put them into the inner dungeon and clamped their feet in the stocks.

Around midnight Paul and Silas were praying and singing hymns to God, and the other prisoners were listening. Suddenly, there was a massive earthquake, and the prison was shaken to its foundations. All the doors immediately flew open, and the chains of every prisoner fell off!

Nothing like this has ever happened to me. But I have been in situations where my life hasn't gone the way I wanted.

When you get to that place in life, you have two choices. You can focus on the bad stuff that's happening or you can focus on the good that God is going to bring out of it.

What's the point?
If you're going through a rough patch, God is still in control, and He knows what is good.

So don't give up because life stinks right now. Instead, choose to rejoice about it, thanking God in advance for what He's going to do.

August 31

Basing worth on what you see

OUR WORLD IS more than what we see. Our lives are more than what we observe. We all have more in common than we think because focusing on our differences is so much easier than trusting what God says.

Galatians 3:28
There is no longer Jew or Gentile, slave or free, male and female. For you are all one in Christ Jesus.

I am a Christ-follower, but my physical self is still an American woman with an English/Scottish heritage. My spiritual self–which is what this verse is about–is beyond all that. My spirit–my soul–isn't physical at all, and it isn't bound to any of the descriptions or labels we need for a human body.

Our souls are beyond our concept of existence. As we are now, we have to label each other so that our differences make sense, but our souls supersede stereotype. Even so, we still put people in boxes and decide who is more valuable than others, based on what we see.

What's the point?
Don't get trapped into thinking that you can stereotype people because of the way they look. They are more than what you see.

Even though we may be different on the outside, our souls have equal worth to God. At first glance, we are all different from each other. But if we are followers of Christ, we all have the Holy Spirit inside.

Knowing that, are you really so different from the person across the room?

September 2015

?

HELP

Asking for help is usually regarded as a sign of being weak. It means you're not strong enough to accomplish something on your own. Or you don't know where you're going. Or you can't get through life without turning to someone else.

The truth is, nobody can make it through life alone. Everyone needs help now and then, and the best person to ask for help is God because He knows what you really need.

September 1

Mountains are only good for looking at

SOMETHING ABOUT difficult times makes everyone eager to talk to God, to tell Him what's bothering us, to explain how we need His help. And that's great. That's what He wants us to do. But I think sometimes we forget that God isn't just waiting to get us out of trouble; He's there to keep us from getting into trouble in the first place.

Psalm 121
I look up to the mountains—
does my help come from there?
My help comes from the Lord,
who made heaven and earth!
He will not let you stumble;
the one who watches over you will not slumber.
Indeed, he who watches over Israel
never slumbers or sleeps.
The Lord himself watches over you!
The Lord stands beside you as your protective shade.
The sun will not harm you by day,
nor the moon at night.
The Lord keeps you from all harm
and watches over your life.
The Lord keeps watch over you as you come and go,
both now and forever.

God never gets tired. He never goes to sleep. Even when the world is full of danger, with God as our help, we can't fail.

What's the point?
Look to God for help. Mountains are beautiful, but when you get right down to it, they're just big rocks. And big rocks don't really do much.

Our help comes from God, who made the mountains. And He's standing beside you waiting to help you through your day.

September 2

Seeking help from God is a journey

SEEKING GOD IS a Christian catch phrase church people drop when they want to sound spiritual. It's a good generic answer for just about any question, but what does it mean?

Seeking God means we need Him with complete and utter humility. If you need someone else, that means you can't get through life without them.

Psalm 69:32
The humble will see their God at work and be glad.
Let all who seek God's help be encouraged.

God rarely answers a request the way you ask Him to. Many times, God's answer will sound like "No" and at that point, we give up and stop asking. But "Not yet" doesn't necessarily mean "No." And that's why you have to keep asking. You have to keep on keeping on until the day when the "Not yet" becomes a "Go for it!"

Seeking God's help is a choice we have to make every day—to keep moving forward in spite of the answers we think we get. And you can be sure that if you get an answer that causes you to rely on yourself, that's not from God. Because if we want God to help us, we have to put our faith and trust in Him completely.

What's the point?
Seeking God's help is a journey that makes us realize how much we really need Him. That those who come to Him seeking His help humbly will be encouraged, because He hears them.

So be encouraged, Seeker. He hears you.

September 3

Joy in asking for help

WHY IS ASKING for help usually thought of in a negative context? Maybe this isn't the case for anyone else, but when I think of asking for help, I think of how the person I'm asking will react. Will they think I'm nagging? Will they wonder why I don't just try to do it myself? Will they think I'm weak? Will I be putting a strain on them financially, emotionally, physically?

All of those things go through my mind, and it's just so much easier and so much simpler to not ask.

Psalm 146:5
But joyful are those who have the God of Israel as their helper, whose hope is in the Lord their God.

When you ask God for help, He doesn't think ill of us. He doesn't think that we should try to do things by ourselves. He wants to help us. It brings Him joy to help us.

What's the point?
Life gets complicated because I make it complicated. I think it just happens because my brain is a complicated place to live. But if you really think about it, life is simple. At least, it should be. Asking for help should be simple too.

When you ask God for help, it is simple. He's the one person who you can never confuse, even with all your intricate complexities. He always has an answer, and He always has a plan, and He always knows exactly what needs to happen. And I don't know about you, but that makes me feel pretty joyful.

September 4

God gives His people strength

LIFE TAKES A lot of work and focus and energy, and some days I run out of all of it. But I don't like asking for help. I don't like admitting that I can't do something on my own, so I'm perfectly content to plug along in my own power until I collapse.

But we aren't supposed to live that way. We were never meant to make it through life on our own strength.

Psalm 29:11
The Lord gives his people strength.
The Lord blesses them with peace.

Can you imagine facing your life's trouble today, armed with God's strength instead of your own?

Read the rest of the Psalm, if you have time. God's voice alone can split the sky, tear massive trees apart, and cause mighty mountains to tremble. Literally. That's just His voice. Imagine what the rest of Him can do. And He offers that strength to us.

What's the point?
It's all right to be tired. We're all human. We all run out of steam. But we don't have to stay exhausted. God is standing by waiting for us to ask for His help.

God has offered His strength to us. And I, for one, intend to take Him up on it. Because coffee, though wonderful, can only accomplish so much. To get through a day when I'm tired to my very core, I need strength that doesn't come from me. And thanks to Jesus, all I have to do to get it is ask for it.

September 7

How paintball showed me teams matter

I DIDN'T GO paintballing until high school. I think we were supposed to be on teams. I prefer to compete alone, because I slow teams down, and that makes me feel guilty. But teams are important in paintballing because when you attack someone, your partner can take them out—before you get shot three times point blank in the chest.

Ouch.

If you've got to charge into battle, you're stupid to go it alone.

Numbers 11:16-17
Then the Lord said to Moses, "Gather before me seventy men who are recognized as elders and leaders of Israel. Bring them to the Tabernacle to stand there with you. I will come down and talk to you there. I will take some of the Spirit that is upon you, and I will put the Spirit upon them also. They will bear the burden of the people along with you, so you will not have to carry it alone."

Moses, regarded as one of the greatest leaders in history, couldn't manage the Israelite nation alone, so God told him to get a team together. And that principle is still good to remember today. Or do you think you can handle your life by yourself?

What's the point?
God has put some amazing people in our lives, and they'd probably be thrilled if you asked them for help. Don't believe Satan's lies that you have to do everything alone. That's not true, and that's not what God intended for you.

Being tough is fine. Being stupid about it? That's something else entirely.

September 8

Asking for better fruit

PRODUCING FRUIT is one of those churchy phrases that used to kind of creep me out when I was little. I thought it meant that if I did things for God, I would be like a fruit tree. I think some part of me expected apples might start popping out of my fingers when I obeyed my parents.

But producing fruit for God is more like helping other people come to know Him or encouraging other believers in their time of need.

Colossians 1:10
Then the way you live will always honor and please the Lord, and your lives will produce every kind of good fruit. All the while, you will grow as you learn to know God better and better.

This verse is interesting to me, because it sounds very much like a process. First, we have to live in a way that will always honor and please the Lord. And as we live that way, our lives will produce every kind of good fruit (not just one kind).

Once you understand God's will and wisdom, knowing how to live in a way that pleases God will be second nature to you.

What's the point?
You won't accomplish great things for God until you live in a way that pleases Him. If living to please God is second nature, producing fruit for God will be effortless.

But it's not just the results you'll gain. You'll also get closer to God, which just makes life better all the way around.

❓ September 9
Ask God for help before you need it

THERE HAVE BEEN times where I didn't receive very good customer service. I came looking for help or looking for answers, and there was no one there to help me. Or the people who were there weren't very helpful. Not only is that irritating, it's discouraging.

Psalm 69:32
The humble will see their God at work and be glad.
Let all who seek God's help be encouraged.

How fortunate are we that God isn't like a lazy customer service person? He's our loving Father who wants to help us and who is infinitely qualified to do so.

Not that He's like a customer service line. God doesn't work like that. Actually, most of the time, He's helping behind the scenes before we even know we need His help.

But God never turns anyone who comes seeking Him away. Not ever. Never once in history has He turned away someone who came seeking Him, no matter who they were or what they did. Anyone who came to Him for help, He helped.

What's the point?
Whatever situation you're in, God can help. He knows what to do. He has an eternity of wisdom to offer. So call Him up and see what He says. You don't have to talk to a computer, and He won't try to sell you anything.

God is waiting for you to ask for His help today. God wants to help us, and we're nuts if we tell Him we can do it ourselves. Because we can't.

September 10

The best Bible study leader

WE THINK WE have to know everything. And when we don't know the answer to something that means we are insufficient in some way. Maybe that's just me and other people don't feel that way. But I don't think so. And we're the same way about the Bible, especially if you've grown up in church.

If you don't know the answer to some random biblical question, it's really easy to think you're lacking something.

Psalm 119:18
Open my eyes to see
the wonderful truths in your instructions.

The Bible isn't difficult to understand, but there are a lot of stories to keep track of. And there is so much inside that you can spend a lifetime and not understand it all.

But you need to start studying Scripture with the understanding that you're not going to grasp it all by yourself. God needs to be studying right along with you, explaining things to you and helping you make sense of everything that's in there.

What's the point?
Don't give up if you can't understand something you read in Scripture. Just ask for help.

And I'm not talking about going to a pastor or a mature believer. You certainly can, but ask God for help first. The Bible will always interpret itself if you let it. Ask Him to reveal another verse to you that will explain what you just read.

Never be ashamed to ask someone for help. At some point, your Christian role model had to ask for help too.

September 11

Just get on the horse

I AM NOT afraid of horses. I just lack experience. So when I had the choice to hike three miles through the Guatemalan jungle to visit a village, I took it, rather than riding the horse. I just didn't expect to dehydrate so quickly.

Once I figured out that I was in trouble, I was too stubborn to just get on the horse anyway, so I kept going, until my equally stubborn traveling companion forced me onto the poor, sagging beast. Looking back, I should have asked for help earlier, but asking for help is something I'm not good at.

Psalm 46:1
God is our refuge and strength,
always ready to help in times of trouble.

That phrase *always ready* can also be translated *very present and well-proved*. How many people can you say are willing to offer help like that? Most of the time, the help people offer is according to their availability or their schedules. But not God. If we ask Him for help, He will help us.

What's the point?
God wants to help us. God wants to be involved in my life, actively working alongside me and helping me through difficult situations.

If I try to get through life on my own, I'm not going to make it. Physically, emotionally, financially—I'll be a wreck. But if I let God lead me, and if I trust Him to help me make the right choices, I can't go wrong.

September 14

The only throne where you can be bold

IN OLDER TIMES, whenever common people needed something from a king or queen, they had to approach the throne and beg for it. I have an active imagination, and I can feel the fear and trepidation something like this might cause. To be so small and so far away from someone so much bigger and more powerful than me would terrify me.

So what happens when we pray?

Hebrews 4:16
So let us come boldly to the throne of our gracious God. There we will receive his mercy, and we will find grace to help us when we need it most.

If you have chosen to follow Jesus, that means you have full access to God Himself. He isn't some distant ethereal being floating out in the universe somewhere who doesn't care about your everyday life. He is a real, living Person who wants to know you and help you.

Think about asking a queen or a president for something you need. Then imagine approaching the throne of the God of the universe. It doesn't even compare. But today's verse is saying that we can walk right up to the throne of God and talk to Him. And we won't be shunned or punished. We'll receive mercy and grace when we need it most.

What's the point?
Be bold. You can. God wants you to.

If you believe in Jesus, you are God's child. That means you can walk boldly up to His throne and tell Him what's going on in your life. And He'll help you.

September 15

Wandering is a waste of your time

I HAVE A terrible sense of direction, but I'd rather find my own way. Would it be easier to ask someone which way I should go? Absolutely. But do I do it? Absolutely not!

I won't even ask for directions in a grocery store. I'd rather find it myself, even if that requires that I spend a lot more time and effort.

Maybe spending too much time looking for peanut butter isn't a big deal, but if you get into the habit of refusing to ask for directions in the small things, it won't be long before you refuse to ask for directions in bigger things.

Psalm 25:12
Who are those who fear the Lord?
He will show them the path they should choose.

Refusing to listen to God is pride. Refusing to accept God's directions, even though they've been made plain to us, is pride. And pride is always dangerous, no matter what form it takes.

If you're refusing to take God at His Word because you think you know better, you're just asking for trouble.

What's the point?
Stop fighting and start listening. God wants the best for us. He's not trying to squash our fun. He just wants to prevent us from making mistakes that will plague us for the rest of our lives.

After all, life is really too short to waste time wandering around the grocery store searching for peanut butter when all you have to do is ask for it.

September 16

Witnessing how God works

EVERYONE HAS PROBABLY had to deal with a situation they can't control. Recently, for once, instead of worrying about it, I decided that I was going to just let God take care of it.

Well, surprise, surprise, He did.

I found out a few weeks later that the problem was taken care of. And not only was it not even an issue anymore, everyone involved was happy about it. And I didn't have to do a single thing. God arranged everything to work out in exactly the way it needed to.

Isaiah 65:24
I will answer them before they even call to me.
While they are still talking about their needs,
I will go ahead and answer their prayers!

Everybody usually expects God to answer prayer after we ask for it. But how cool is it to know that sometimes God answers your prayers before you even ask?

If God answers your prayer after you ask, it's amazing. It's the most amazing experience to know that He's listening. But what will really blow your mind is how He works things out before you even know they're going wrong. And He does that all the time.

What's the point?
Don't be afraid to ask. He knows what you need, but He wants to hear you ask for it.

Half the time, I'm convinced we don't realize we need it until we ask. And then He's there to gently bop us on the head and remind us that He's got everything under control … and that He always has.

September 17

Christian cannibalism

THE CHURCH WAS founded to reach out to the lost, to support believers, to provide a safe place to worship and learn and grow. Sadly, in my experiences, the church in America is less like a support base and more like a tank of piranhas. Piranhas will devour any other fish who happens to come along and doesn't fit in, and in difficult circumstances, they will devour each other too.

Romans 14:13
So let's stop condemning each other. Decide instead to live in such a way that you will not cause another believer to stumble and fall.

Christians are terrible about condemning each other. Another believer puts a toe out of line, and instantly they become public enemy number one.

They are shunned. They are spoken ill of. Everyone around them treats them like they have leprosy. And that's not the vision Christ had for the Church.

Now, do we let sin go? No, of course, not. There are times and places to hold each other accountable. But there has to be a point where we in the church focus less on finding fault in other believers and focusing more on how we live our own lives instead.

What's the point?
Care more about the mistakes and choices you are making, rather than finding fault in another believer.

God has called us to help each other, not attack. If your brother or sister in Christ needs help, help them. Don't point fingers. Don't accuse. Be to them who Jesus is to you.

September 19

Living undefeated by standing still

IF YOU WANT to live a life that God can use in a big way, He's going to drop you in some situations that are out of your depth. You're going to feel like the least qualified person in the world. You're going to fear making mistakes that will damage your future and the future of the people around you. You're going to want to play it safe, and I'm telling you right now: Don't.

Exodus 14:13-14
But Moses told the people, "Don't be afraid. Just stand still and watch the Lord rescue you today. The Egyptians you see today will never be seen again. The Lord himself will fight for you. Just stay calm."

This is what Moses said to the Children of Israel shortly before God parted the Red Sea. Pharaoh's army was closing in on them. They had no escape. I don't blame them for despairing. It was too much for them to handle. But what none of them realized at the time is that the battle wasn't theirs to fight in the first place.

God Himself fought for the Children of Israel, and they didn't have to do anything. They just had to stand still and be calm and watch. And, Christians, that's where we are today too.

What's the point?

If you are a Christ-follower, your life isn't your own, so why would this fight be yours too? Yeah, show up. Yeah, be strong, but you don't have to stand in the ring.

Stand still. God Himself will fight for you, and He is undefeated.

? September 21

Backstage

I WORKED BACKSTAGE on dramas for years, and that's where I love to be. The backstage is the well-oiled machine that keeps a show running. Yes, your actors can be phenomenal. And your director can be visionary. And your writing can win awards.

But backstage is invisible. It's there to help the actors and the directors and the writers shine, while receiving little to no credit at all.

Matthew 6:2-4.
When you give to someone in need, don't do as the hypocrites do—blowing trumpets in the synagogues and streets to call attention to their acts of charity! I tell you the truth, they have received all the reward they will ever get. But when you give to someone in need, don't let your left hand know what your right hand is doing. Give your gifts in private, and your Father, who sees everything, will reward you.

People who help others in order to draw attention to their good works are hypocrites. That's what the religious people of Jesus' day did. They wanted to make sure everyone knew that they were sacrificing to help people around them.

But what Jesus is saying here is that when you help someone, you shouldn't make a big deal out of it. You should keep it private. You should keep it between you and God.

What's the point?
When it comes to helping others, stick to the backstage. Don't desire adulation or credit, and don't seek after the spotlight.

God knows what's going on in your heart, and He will make sure you receive the reward you deserve for your actions.

September 22

Being nice is not enough

SOMETIMES I READ Proverbs, and they don't sound right. Like the writer took two completely unrelated sentences and joined them together with a comma and coordinating conjunction and expected people to get the point. But as a grammar fiend, it irks me because compound sentences are supposed to be composed of two closely related sentences.

But God knows grammar rules. So if a verse out of Proverbs sounds mashed together and unrelated, I'm not reading it right.

Proverbs 16:21
The wise are known for their understanding,
and pleasant words are persuasive.

If I were writing this verse, I would have written this differently. Because being known for understanding and persuading with pleasant words don't sound related at all. Pleasant words are nice, sure, but persuasive? Most of the time when I need something and try to be pleasant about it, I don't end up persuading anyone.

Pleasant words by themselves aren't enough, but pleasant words wielded by a wise person? Now that's a dangerous combination.

If you have wisdom, you can communicate on every level. Understanding means you "get people." And if you get people, you know how to talk to them. You don't have to insult or browbeat or attack. You can be pleasant.

What's the point?
Wisdom and pleasant words are powerful tools. They are persuasive, yes, but implementing them at the same time will make a huge difference in your work environment.

If you use wisdom and pleasantness together, you might be surprised at what you can accomplish.

September 23

Look for the chance to do good

IT'S EASY TO talk about being nice to others. It's not as easy to actually do it. Being nice to other people takes effort, especially if you've had a bad day. But the Bible clearly says in more than one place that we need to be kind to each other, and it's not just talking about Christians being kind to Christians. Christians need to be kind to nonbelievers. Christians, we need to be kind to everyone.

Galatians 6:10
Therefore, whenever we have the opportunity, we should do good to everyone—especially to those in the family of faith.

Whenever you have the chance to do good for someone, do it. And I love how Paul emphasizes the part about doing good to other believers.

Sometimes being kind to other believers is the most difficult. But the way Christians treat each other is supposed to show the world that we're different.

What's the point?

Keep your eyes peeled for someone you can help. You can hold doors for people. You can help people carry groceries or take their cart to the return bin. You can smile at someone in line. You can speak kindly to the stressed-out college student in the drive-thru. You can watch for the opportunity to be an encouragement to someone else.

Negativity may be contagious, but the best way to fight it is to look for opportunities to brighten people's lives.

September 24

Helping others responsibly

I LOVE TO help people. And I know a lot of other people like that too. There's something cathartic, I think, in serving other people. It gets your focus off yourself and reminds you how blessed you are. Besides that, it's just fun. And it's even more fun if you can help people in a group. But there's a difference between helping people and enabling people.

Romans 15:2
We should help others do what is right and build them up in the Lord.

When we help someone else, we need to make sure that we're helping other people to do what is right. There is a difference between helping someone change a tire when it's 10 degrees outside and helping someone buy school books when they've spent all their money on clothes.

What's the point?
Helping people is good. It's not only good; it's a commandment. And it's fun, remember? But we have to make sure we're helping people do the right thing. Because if we are consciously enabling people to do wrong, to live a life that isn't pleasing to God, we will be the ones responsible.

Yes, the person you help, who is actually making the poor choices, will be responsible for his or her own actions. But aren't we responsible for our choices too?

Helping people who want to help themselves is right. Helping people who want you to do all the work for them is a very bad idea.

How to deal with a heart problem

I DON'T LIKE being wrong. And I don't like being corrected. I get stiff and irritated when someone tells me that I'm wrong. It's 100% pride, and I recognize it. It's been a constant battle my whole life to be humble when it comes to facing my own flaws. But it's one thing to point out your own flaws. It's something else for someone else to see them and mention them.

Psalm 139:23-24
Search me, O God, and know my heart;
test me and know my anxious thoughts.
Point out anything in me that offends you,
and lead me along the path of everlasting life.

I'm not sure if I can pray this honestly. It's one thing to be wrong. It's another thing to invite God to tell me what I'm wrong about.

The point of us asking Him to search us is to come to terms with His absolute holiness, realizing our own smallness and our own insignificance in the face of His perfection. When we are open with the darkness of our lives before God, it makes us understand just how unworthy of His love we are.

What's the point?
Instead of trying to hide what's wrong, ask God to look. Ask Him to reveal the parts of your life that have no place, because when He brings those things to light, He also shows us the way to leave them behind.

Open your heart to God today. Let Him see what's inside. He loves you, and He won't change His mind. On the contrary, He'll change yours.

? September 28

Who has your back?

SOME CHRISTIANS TALK about God like He's crouching in heaven with a sledgehammer, just waiting to smash us the instant we step out of line. I know Christians who believe that. I know Christians who live like that. And, to be honest, I lived that way for a little while—until I learned better.

It makes sense to us that God would be ready to point out everything we've done wrong, and He could. But He's much more interested in helping us out instead.

Psalm 86:5
O Lord, you are so good, so ready to forgive,
so full of unfailing love for all who ask for your help.

I'm so thankful that we serve a God who forgives us, not a tyrant in the sky intent on pummeling us or crushing us. But God even goes a step further beyond just forgiving us. He also wants to help us.

The thought of that takes my breath away. God, the Creator of the universe, wants to help me with my problems. That's incredible! And all I need to do is ask.

What's the point?
We don't have to worry because when we ask, God will help. When we ask Him for help, He's excited to help us.

He's watching out for us and waiting for the moment when we get it through our thick heads that we can't do it alone. And when we finally let go of our stupid, foolish pride, He's right there. He's got us covered.

? September 29

God will use someone but maybe not you

SELFLESS PEOPLE are heroes. And I find it ironic that the most selfless people I know aren't wealthy. They're just average people willing to give God their limited resources.

1 Kings 17:9-13
So he [Elijah] went to Zarephath. As he arrived at the gates of the village, he saw a widow gathering sticks, and he asked her, "Would you please bring me a little water in a cup?" As she was going to get it, he called to her, "Bring me a bite of bread, too."

But she said, "I swear by the Lord your God that I don't have a single piece of bread in the house. And I have only a handful of flour left in the jar and a little cooking oil in the bottom of the jug. I was just gathering a few sticks to cook this last meal, and then my son and I will die."

But Elijah said to her, "Don't be afraid! Go ahead and do just what you've said, but make a little bread for me first. Then use what's left to prepare a meal for yourself and your son."

This poor widow had nothing, but because she was willing to help Elijah, God provided enough food for her and her son to outlast the drought.

What would have happened if she had refused? Well, she and her son would have starved. And God would have used someone else to provide for Elijah.

What's the point?
You can't give God so much that He can't pay you back. Someone in your life needs something from you, and you can choose to help them or not.

But before you make that choice remember God can use anyone.

September 30

Say thanks before the joy fades

GOD, THE INVENTOR of the sunrise, the shaper of the universe, the genius behind the duck-billed platypus, listens to our requests and always answers. And He doesn't just answer; many times, He answers personally. It's like getting the perfect Christmas gift from someone who knows you better than you know yourself.

I've got the joy part down. What I sometimes forget is the thanksgiving part.

Psalm 28:7
The Lord is my strength and shield.
I trust him with all my heart.
He helps me, and my heart is filled with joy.
I burst out in songs of thanksgiving.

Joy is great. And understanding the concept of Someone like God paying attention to our requests is beyond awesome. But let's not take it for granted. We need to make sure He knows that we're thankful.

What's the point?

Tell God what you're thankful for. He wants to hear. Yes, He knows if you're thankful, but something happens when you tell people you're thankful. It's a humility thing. It deepens your relationship because you're admitting that someone else did something for you that you might not have done for yourself.

So tell Him. He's waiting to hear from you. Don't let that joy you felt when you realized the answer came from Him fade away. Do it now.

October 2015

DEALING WITH
DISCOURAGEMENT

We all face times in our lives when we are discouraged. Maybe you've been trying for years to get a certain job or to achieve a certain goal, and nothing is changing. Maybe you've lost everything you owned. Maybe someone you love turned against you. Or maybe you're just tired.

Whatever the reason, you don't have to live in discouragement. God has given us the answers we need in Scripture to fight through the dark moments in our lives.

So often, discouragement stems from the way we see life. Our task is to learn to see life the way God sees it.

October 1

Why I should not be discouraged

WE ALL KNOW fear is a choice, but a relationship with God means more than just choosing not to be afraid. It means we can choose not to be discouraged too.

Isaiah 41:10
Don't be afraid, for I am with you. Don't be discouraged, for I am your God. I will strengthen you and help you. I will hold you up with my victorious right hand.

God doesn't always answer our questions in a way that we expect. Half the time, He'll answer with a question. And the rest of the time, He'll answer the question we don't even know we're asking. He knows our hearts, and He knows what we need to hear, especially when we don't know. And He's always right.

Question: Why shouldn't I be discouraged? Answer: I am your God.

For me, discouragement comes when I've failed. For me, it's a response to my inadequacy. And when I think about it that way, it suddenly makes sense. My shortcomings are no surprise to Him. God is with me in the good times as well as the bad times.

What's the point?
Life isn't about my failures or my successes. It's about God and what God is doing.

I'm a part of His plan because He put me there–right where He wants me–and nothing is going to happen that He didn't already know about. And when I fail–and I will–I don't need to give in to discouragement because He's my God, and He never leaves people behind.

October 2

Choosing to rejoice

WHEN SOMETHING REALLY wonderful happens, what do you do? You celebrate! At least, you should. Truly, really wonderful things don't happen often enough in this world to not celebrate. But what happens the rest of the time? When life happens, do you celebrate? Probably not. But that doesn't mean you can't still rejoice.

Romans 12:12
Rejoice in our confident hope. Be patient in trouble, and keep on praying.

When the Bible tells us to rejoice, it means that we are supposed to choose to celebrate God's goodness even when we don't feel like it. That's usually where I end up on the spectrum.

I'm exhausted. I'm stressed out. I'm worn down with waiting, and even though I've gotten some answers, they weren't the answers I wanted. So how can I rejoice about all of that? Any rejoicing I do for any of that is likely to come off as half-hearted or sarcastic, and I don't think God would appreciate that.

But there's one thing we can rejoice over whether life is good or not, and that is our confident hope. Our confident hope is in the Lord, whether we have everything or nothing.

So if you've had a great week, rejoice. If you don't get what you want, and all you really want to do is stay in bed, choose to rejoice anyway.

What's the point?
If your hope is in Christ, it's confident, even if you don't feel like it is.

And that means, you can choose to rejoice.

October 5

How much do you trust God?

ARE YOU DISCOURAGED because the world has lost its mind? Lawmakers who should know better are calling good things bad and bad things good. Innocent lives are taken cruelly, and sometimes the law even protects the people who do wrong. Rebellion of every kind runs rampant, and just by standing up for what God says is right, Christ-followers run the risk of persecution.

It could be discouraging, if we let it.

1 Peter 4:19
So if you are suffering in a manner that pleases God, keep on doing what is right, and trust your lives to the God who created you, for he will never fail you.

Do you trust God enough to lose everything? It's not a cheerful question, and it certainly isn't an encouraging question. But it's necessary to ask, because the world isn't getting better, and soon suffering for Christ may not be something that only happens overseas.

The day is coming where those who stand with God won't be able to stay quiet. We will all have to make a public choice. And if you're with the side that follows Christ, you should expect the consequences to be harsh. But one thing you can know for sure is that if you re suffering for God, you won't do it alone.

What's the point?
If you're suffering for God, don't give up. He's told us what's right and what He expects, and we need to trust Him enough to live that way, regardless of what the world says.

He's never failed before, and He won't stop now.

October 6

Focus on the solution, not the problem

DETAILS OVERWHELM me. If there are five major problems staring me in the face, I might get a little stressed, but it's nothing I can't handle. If you throw 30 little things at me simultaneously, I will shut down. That's what happens to me in life—I get bogged down by the problems instead of the solutions.

Psalm 42:11
Why am I discouraged?
Why is my heart so sad?
I will put my hope in God!
I will praise him again—
my Savior and my God!

The world is full of details. Tiny little details that if you miss just one, you can make a terrible mess. But if you start focusing on those details, you're liable to end up living with a very narrow-minded view of the world. When I start focusing on all the tiny little problems I'm facing, that's when I get discouraged.

No matter what problem you're facing, there is a solution to it. You can either choose to focus on how much you have left to do, or you can choose to focus on how you are going to fix it.

What's the point?
In life, you can choose to focus on your inadequacies and all the things you've done wrong, or you can choose to focus on the fact that God never makes mistakes. He's big enough to turn your screw-ups into something that will glorify Him and bless you.

Don't be discouraged. Change your focus.

October 7

The greatest weapon our enemy has

EVERY STORY HAS bad guys who try to stop the good guys from winning. Every tactic they take usually has one unifying purpose–to discourage them. But the irony of that tactic is that heroes overcome obstacles. That's what makes them heroes.

Psalm 19:7-8
The instructions of the Lord are perfect,
reviving the soul.
The decrees of the Lord are trustworthy,
making wise the simple.
The commandments of the Lord are right,
bringing joy to the heart.
The commands of the Lord are clear,
giving insight for living.

Christ-followers have an enemy, and it's not nonbelievers or other religions. It's not any person you can see face to face. No, our enemy is far more deceptive than that. Our enemy is a fallen angel, Satan, who hates God and hates everything God loves. And that includes us. But his tactics are the same as any other enemy in any other story–distraction and discouragement.

For me, it's my emotions. If Satan can twist my emotions and discourage me, I'm much more likely to get off track.

What's the point?
Don't trust what you feel. Trust what God has told you. God's Word is the best weapon you have to fight the discouragement our enemy throws at you. So use them. Remember what God has done for you. Mark it down, and the next time Satan comes after you, shove it in his face in Jesus' name.

Just celebrate. Because if you've got obstacles, that means you're human. If you overcome them, that makes you a hero.

October 8

Facing discouragement with a question

SOMETIMES LIFE feels like it's all wrong. In some instances, we really do make our own trouble. The issues we're facing in life sometimes stem from our own bad choices, but that's not always the case. The world is just broken. People are just broken, and there's no other explanation for it. And, what's worse, there's nothing you can do to fix it.

So what do you do when you reach the point in life where everything around you is breaking and none of it is within your power to repair?

Psalm 43:5
Why am I discouraged?
Why is my heart so sad?
I will put my hope in God!
I will praise him again—
my Savior and my God!

Why are you discouraged? Why is your heart sad? They're not rhetorical questions. God wants to know. He wants you to tell Him what has happened in your life to make you so sad. So tell Him.

Even my great big problems are nothing compared to God and His power and His grace. God can fix anything. God can help me accomplish anything.

What's the point?
Ask yourself why you feel discouraged today. Then tell God about it.

As you tell Him, just remember who He is and who we are to Him, and remember that there's nothing He can't do. Put your hope in God, and praise Him for being who He is. He's got a plan, and it's good.

October 9

Never fear your troubles

GOD HAS A plan for everything, so that means no coincidences. The place we work, the people we meet, the circumstances we encounter–it's all a part of something bigger, and there's a reason for it. The difficult part is remembering that fact.

2 Corinthians 1:3-4
All praise to God, the Father of our Lord Jesus Christ. God is our merciful Father and the source of all comfort. He comforts us in all our troubles so that we can comfort others. When they are troubled, we will be able to give them the same comfort God has given us.

Life has trouble, and each of us is going to hit bumps that will trip us. But those problems don't have to mark the end of our lives. Those troubles will teach you how good God is, how faithful and how awesome. Those things will help your faith grow so big, so strong that nothing can shake your trust in God.

And then, you'll meet someone down the road who is going through the same problem you have, and you'll have the opportunity–the responsibility–to reach out and tell your story. Because if God can be faithful to you, He can be faithful to anyone.

What's the point?
Don't scorn the trouble in your life. Don't run away from it. And don't get angry at God. He's going to help you through it, and after He does, you're going to know Him so much better than before. And then, you can help other people get to know Him too.

October 12

Fight discouragement with praise

LIFE IS KIND of like a yard full of snow drifts. You don't always know how deep they are, and if you aren't careful you can end up stuck.

Isaiah 12:4-5
In that wonderful day you will sing:
"Thank the Lord! Praise his name!
Tell the nations what he has done.
Let them know how mighty he is!
Sing to the Lord, for he has done wonderful things.
Make known his praise around the world.

We don't have to live with discouragement, and God has given us all sorts of weapons to use in the fight against it. My favorite is praise. Praise is hard on a good day, let alone on a day when you feel lower than low, but praise is one of the best things to do when you don't feel like it.

Worship takes your eyes off yourself and puts them on God.

What's the point?
Maybe life stinks right now, but it could be worse. You should always be able to find something positive about it with God's help. Our lives are never as bad as they could be, and that's God's grace.

So in those moments when you end up stuck in the snow drifts, step back and praise God. Focus all your energy on telling Him how great He is, on telling others How great He is, instead of how difficult your life is at the moment, and something miraculous will happen. Your situation won't change, but the way you see it will.

October 13

Fight discouragement with truth

EVERYTHING IN LIFE often seems to go wrong at the same time. Most of the time I can stay focused and remember that God has everything under control. But the rest of the time I just keep marching like a good little soldier, not really feeling it, just trying to put one foot in front of the other and not think about everything that's going wrong.

But is that the way we're supposed to face discouragement? Ignore it? Deny it? Is that the "good Christian" thing to do?

Psalm 59:16
But as for me, I will sing about your power.
Each morning I will sing with joy about your unfailing love.
For you have been my refuge,
a place of safety when I am in distress.

Discouragement is a paralytic. Other feelings can spur you to action, but discouragement slows you down, feeds on your insecurity, and mocks your efforts to fight back. The chief lie that discouragement tells you is that you're alone and that nobody cares about your problems. Discouragement requires isolation so that no one can set you straight.

The best way to fight discouragement is to find someone you trust, someone you love, someone who loves you enough to help you challenge the lies that have convinced you that you'll always fail. And the best person to help you do that is God.

What's the point?
When you feel discouraged, start by talking to God about it. Tell Him what you're feeling.

Take your discouragement to God and let Him help you see what's true and what's not. Then, hold to what's true.

October 14

Define yourself

EVERYONE HAS TALENT, and it's only natural to build a life on those talents. But if you let your talents define you, when you fail at something you're supposed to be good at, you'll see it as a personal attack and not a learning opportunity.

Ephesians 2:13-14
But now you have been united with Christ Jesus. Once you were far away from God, but now you have been brought near to him through the blood of Christ. For Christ himself has brought peace to us. He united Jews and Gentiles into one people when, in his own body on the cross, he broke down the wall of hostility that separated us.

Thanks to Christ, it doesn't matter where you were born or what kind of job you have. If you believe in Him, you are part of His family, citizens of God's kingdom. That's where your identity should come from. If you're a Christ-follower, you're a child of God.

What's the point?
Ask yourself who you are. And if God isn't the source of that definition, something's wrong. Your religion shouldn't define you. Your job shouldn't define you. The only person who has the right to define you is God.

So if you don't know who you are, ask Him.

He'll tell you that you are loved. And once you accept that, you can do anything. You can face any challenge, any discouragement, any problem, and they won't be able to slow you down because your identity comes from Someone who never changes.

October 15

God is bigger than your storm

THE WORLD IS full of storms, both literal and figurative, but the difference between an actual storm and a stormy season in your life is that usually you can take shelter from real wind and rain and hail. And a stormy season of life is something you really can't escape. It follows you everywhere.

It's almost like you have your own black cloud hanging over your head, and there's nothing you can do to get away from it. It just follows you around, dumping rain on you constantly.

John 16:33
I have told you all this so that you may have peace in me. Here on earth you will have many trials and sorrows. But take heart, because I have overcome the world."

When we encounter storms in our lives, it's easy to lose hope. When you're in the middle of a storm, it doesn't feel like anything can be beautiful ever again, and it doesn't feel like anything has a purpose at all.

But what we should never forget is that God is bigger than our storms. Yes, a storm can cause immense damage and can take precious lives, but God is strong enough to help us through it.

What's the point?
God can overcome any trouble we face, and for those who belong to Him, we don't need to fear the world or anything in it.

God is bigger than the world's problems, and He's strong enough to take disaster and make it beautiful.

October 16

Hope is dangerous

HOPE IS SOMETHING we all need to make it through life, but can you guarantee that what you hope for will happen? Can you trust the source of your hope? Like faith, hope is a choice. It's something you choose to do moment after moment. But hope can be dangerous if it's misplaced.

Jeremiah 17:7-8
"But blessed are those who trust in the Lord
and have made the Lord their hope and confidence.
They are like trees planted along a riverbank,
with roots that reach deep into the water.
Such trees are not bothered by the heat
or worried by long months of drought.
Their leaves stay green,
and they never stop producing fruit.

You have to be careful where you place your hope. If you have placed your hope in your education or your accomplishments, in your wealth or possessions, you're in trouble. Those things will eventually fade. Even people will eventually let you down. Hope is dangerous when you place it in something that doesn't last or in a source that you can't trust.

What's the point?
If you draw hope from God, from Christ, from what is written in Scripture, you'll be like a tree by a clean, pure river that grows strong and tall with deep roots. In bad storms, you won't fall. And during times of intense discomfort, you'll still be able to do what God created you to do.

Choose to put your hope in God.

October 19

Never give up

OUR ENEMY WILL do anything to discourage us, even use us against each other.

Satan wants us to focus the sum of our disappointment and our fears and our loneliness on each other. Since he can't separate us from God, he will manipulate us and use us to hurt each other. And sometimes we're so good at rationalizing it's easy to think we're doing something good, when we're really just playing into his hands.

Micah 7:7-8
As for me, I look to the Lord for help.
I wait confidently for God to save me,
and my God will certainly hear me.
Do not gloat over me, my enemies!
For though I fall, I will rise again.
Though I sit in darkness,
the Lord will be my light.

The darkest times in my life have come in the moments when people I love have hurt me. Maybe they meant well, but a careless word or a selfish deed turned their good intentions into a knife in my back. It's so important to check every word, every thought against Scripture. Otherwise, you run the risk of causing damage instead of preventing it.

What's the point?

God is our help. He's the source of our hope, and He will save us. But that doesn't mean we won't go through some pain, even at the expense of people we love.

No matter who knocks you down, remember that God is the one who holds you up.

October 20

God never gives up on us

EVERY CHRISTIAN I know identifies with Peter. He was all impulse and instinct, shooting his mouth off and putting his foot in it too. Peter has a reputation in Scripture for screwing up, honestly. If he wasn't scolding children, he was chopping off people's ears. But Peter got one thing right. Peter knew Who Jesus was.

And that's something many Christians don't realize.

Matthew 16:15-16
Then he asked them, "But who do you say I am?" Simon Peter answered, "You are the Messiah, the Son of the living God."

Jesus makes people uncomfortable. He is not (and never will be) a neutral presence. You can't just ignore Him, although some people try really hard. Peter had it right. Jesus is the Messiah. He was in the first century. He is today, in the twenty-first century. And we don't need to be afraid of standing up and declaring that fact when we believe it.

The funny thing is, I think Peter really did believe it. However, when he was pressed, he denied it. But when it was over, and after Jesus had come back to life, He tracked Peter down and made sure Peter understood that He still loved him. And from that moment on, Peter became a powerhouse, and he never looked back.

What's the point?
Even when we aren't as bold about our faith as we should be, Jesus still loves us. And He still has plenty of purpose for our lives.

The only thing that can come between you and God's plan is you.

October 21

God is not finished with you yet

PART OF FOLLOWING Christ that is difficult for me is believing that He's still working when all the doors of opportunity have shut in my face.

Philippians 1:6
And I am certain that God, who began the good work within you, will continue his work until it is finally finished on the day when Christ Jesus returns.

God has plans for all of us, and He's promised that He'll see them through to completion. Following Christ is a process, and you learn something new about God every step of the way.

God has promised that what He started in your heart on the day you accepted Christ is a process that won't be finished until Christ comes back for us.

But I think it refers to our dreams too. God gives everyone a dream. Even if you've ignored it to the point that you've forgotten what it was, you had a dream. God gave it to you. And God never gives us anything without a purpose. The difficulty comes in realizing that the fulfillment of our dreams won't always look like what we expect.

What's the point?
Don't give up on God. Maybe your life circumstances are all working together to discourage you. Maybe people you trusted have turned against you. Maybe you think you're out of opportunities to try again. Or maybe you're just so tired you can't keep going.

Your dream is still alive, and God's not finished with you yet. Keep trusting because He can see how all the pieces fit.

October 22

Disappointment can make you stronger

I DON'T DO sports. But then, I'd never had a team I cared about make it to a place where I could cheer them on until recently. I'm a proud alum of Wichita State University, so even though I don't really care about sports, I still pay attention when our sports teams accomplish great things. Everyone knows how that game went in 2014. Undefeated—and then BOOM!

But the Shockers haven't given up basketball just because they didn't win the tournament. Instead, they used their defeat to learn how to be stronger.

Psalm 73:1-3
Truly God is good to Israel,
to those whose hearts are pure.
But as for me, I almost lost my footing.
My feet were slipping, and I was almost gone.
For I envied the proud
when I saw them prosper despite their wickedness.

You will face disappointment in life. The world is broken, and nobody is perfect. Dreams don't always come true, and even though you work your butt off to accomplish something, you may not receive the reward for it right away.

Life is all about perspective. You really do win some and lose some, and on the days that you lose, you have to pick yourself up and keep moving forward. Don't give up. Don't look back. And keep trying until you make it.

What's the point?
Disappointment isn't wrong. It isn't even bad.

Disappointment can make us stronger if we see it as God giving us an opportunity to do something better than we planned.

October 23

Following God is not about incentives

SOMETIMES I WISH God would just tell me what He wants me to do. Or if He won't do that, I want some kind of confirmation that I'm doing the right thing–a confirmation that sticks around instead of popping up momentarily and then vanishing without a trace. I've felt like the donkey God is leading around with a carrot, promising great things but only delivering disappointment. And maybe you'd never say that out loud, but you've felt it before too.

Hebrews 10:23
Let us hold tightly without wavering to the hope we affirm, for God can be trusted to keep his promise.

It's not wrong to look for signs of affirmation, and it's not wrong to do something for God because He's promised something in return. But the danger in focusing on signs or incentives is that we begin to make them the point of following God, and they aren't.

We're not supposed to take great leaps of faith because God will reward us financially or in some other quantifiable, measurable return. And I'm not saying that's not true. But should we be doing God's work for the sole purpose of a return on our investment?

What's the point?
Following God isn't about the incentives. Stop worrying about what you're going to get out of it and just walk with God.

His promises aren't flights of fancy or caprice that He forgets whenever it suits Him. No, when He makes a promise, we can trust that He will keep it.

October 26

Need to see God today?

HAS SOMEONE encouraged you when you were down? Or let you blow off steam without criticizing? Has someone told you they love you with no ulterior motive?

Behavior like that isn't compulsory. Just because you are friends or family or Christians doesn't mean they will go the extra mile to show you much they love you. But people filled with God's love can't help but share it with others.

1 John 4:11-12
Dear friends, since God loved us that much, we surely ought to love each other. No one has ever seen God. But if we love each other, God lives in us, and his love is brought to full expression in us.

Are you looking for God? Look at the Christ-followers in your life. If they love you and sacrifice for you, what do you think could make another stubborn, selfish human being actually want to do that for another person? That's right. God's love. God's love for us overflows so that we have too much to handle and have to give it away.

What's the point?
When I'm feeling down and I want to see God so I know I'm going the right direction, invariably someone comes across my path to encourage me–and they have no reason to.

If you need to see God, watch people who love Him, and you'll see undeniable proof of God through the love His people have for each other.

October 27

The wait is worth it

ANYONE WHO TELLS you life isn't about waiting is lying. Some days, it feels like that's all life is. Waiting. When you're a kid, you are waiting for the day you can drive a car. When you're old enough to drive, you're waiting for the day you're "grown up enough" to live on your own. When you're out on your own, you're waiting for the right person so you don't have to be alone. You get the idea. But it seems to work that way in our walk with Christ too.

Hebrews 6:13-15
For example, there was God's promise to Abraham. Since there was no one greater to swear by, God took an oath in his own name, saying: "I will certainly bless you, and I will multiply your descendants beyond number." Then Abraham waited patiently, and he received what God had promised.

God made promises to Abraham. Ridiculous, impossible promises. And Abraham had to live a good deal of life before he even got to see some of those promises kept. He actually died before most of God's promises came true. Even so, Abraham believed God would keep His promises. And God did, even though Abraham didn't always hold up his end of the deal.

What's the point?
Whatever you're waiting on, don't despair. You may have to sit still, but God is never still. He's always working on something. And there are no better hands to leave your problems in. He has unlimited resources, unlimited time, and unlimited love, and He wants what's best for you.

October 28

Everyday courage

THERE HAVE BEEN points in my life where I feel like I have failed so miserably that it's not worth getting up in the morning. But I can't stop moving. God has too much for me to do. So instead of using my own strength, I used His.

1 Samuel 30:6
David was now in great danger because all his men were very bitter about losing their sons and daughters, and they began to talk of stoning him. But David found strength in the Lord his God.

When David faced his men — his brothers in arms — knowing that they were angry with him for the loss of their families, the only way he could continue to lead was to take strength from God.

On dark days, you need courage to move forward, but it's not flashy courage. It's quiet courage, the kind of courage that keeps you moving forward when all you really want to do is give up. That kind of courage often goes unnoticed. Or it's mistaken for faith or perseverance, and that's what it is to a certain extent.

But if you're going to endure through difficult times without being able to see what's at the end of the road, you have to have courage. Maybe it's everyday courage, but it's still courage.

What's the point?
Draw on God's strength today and be courageous. Maybe not battlefield courageous but everyday courageous, and God will give you victory.

God isn't going anywhere. He hasn't left you. And He's standing ready to help whenever you call.

October 29

Fear does not always roar

FEAR IS OUR default. People don't have to learn how to be afraid. It's part of being human, and it's diametrically opposed to the kind of life God wants us to live.

But fear doesn't always roar. Most of the time it's a lot quieter, like a whisper that you can't stop listening to no matter how much you try.

Psalm 46:1-3
God is our refuge and strength,
always ready to help in times of trouble.
So we will not fear when earthquakes come
and the mountains crumble into the sea.
Let the oceans roar and foam.
Let the mountains tremble as the waters surge!

Fear is a sneaky little problem that can creep into every area of our lives without us even knowing it's there. Maybe it's a quiet fear, but it's still fear. And any kind of fear — whether it's fear of the world or fear of our circumstances — cripples us.

What's the point?
God wants to use us. He's got awesome plans for us, and He wants to work in our lives in miraculous ways. But if we give in to our fear, we aren't going to seize the opportunities He sends our way.

God wants to bless us. And we can't let fear guide us. If we do, we'll only end up wandering around in the dark.

October 30

No wonder my heart is glad

WE HAVE A lot to be thankful for. Even on our worst day, we still
have more than enough good in our lives that we should be thankful.
It's human nature to focus on the negative, but if you follow Christ,
you aren't subject to your human nature. You have two natures now,
and you also have a choice of which one to listen to.

Psalm 16:1, 5, 9
Keep me safe, O God,
for I have come to you for refuge.
Lord, you alone are my inheritance, my cup of blessing.
You guard all that is mine.
No wonder my heart is glad, and I rejoice.

God is our refuge and our protection, but He's more than that. God is
our joy. He is our future and our heritage all at the same time. And
the good things He has given us now pale in comparison to what's
coming. And as we wait for that day, He won't leave us. Ever.

No wonder David's heart was glad. And our hearts should feel the
same way.

What's the point?
Your attitude determines your perspective, and if you're only
listening to your fallen nature, all you'll see is the negative side of
every situation.

Instead of listening to what the world says, focus on what the Bible
says. Step back and look at your life honestly the next time you feel
grumpy and start making a list of everything you have that God gave
you. The length of the list might surprise you.

November 2015

GRATITUDE

November is known as the month to be thankful. We all take the time to stop and focus on being thankful, whether it's among our families or on outlets like social media. It's great to thank the people who've been kind to you or who have done nice things for you, but how often do you stop and thank God for what He's done in your life?

But gratitude toward God should happen more than just one month out of a year. It should be a lifestyle.

November 2

You never know but God does

LIFE DOESN'T ALWAYS go the way you want it to. Sometimes you end up stuck in situations you would never have chosen, and you didn't do anything to deserve them. Life just happened.

But when was the last time you thanked God because life fell apart?

Isaiah 55:8-11
"My thoughts are nothing like your thoughts," says the Lord.
"And my ways are far beyond anything you could imagine.
For just as the heavens are higher than the earth,
so my ways are higher than your ways
and my thoughts higher than your thoughts.
The rain and snow come down from the heavens
and stay on the ground to water the earth.
They cause the grain to grow,
producing seed for the farmer
and bread for the hungry.
It is the same with my word.
I send it out, and it always produces fruit.
It will accomplish all I want it to,
and it will prosper everywhere I send it."

What's the point?

When something bad happens to you, the way you react to it will set the tone of the circumstance as a whole. You can treat it like a curse, like a problem, like a punishment. Or you can treat it like an opportunity to get to know God better. The way you tackle trials in your life makes all the difference in the world.

Horrible things happen in life, but just because a situation looks bad now doesn't mean that it will always be bad.

November 3

We can be content where we are

IT'S GOOD TO control the things you can control, and it's good to do your best. But you shouldn't go to extremes with either because you'll crash. That usually doesn't stop us from trying, though.

Philippians 4:10-12
How I praise the Lord that you are concerned about me again. I know you have always been concerned for me, but you didn't have the chance to help me.

Not that I was ever in need, for I have learned how to be content with whatever I have. I know how to live on almost nothing or with everything. I have learned the secret of living in every situation, whether it is with a full stomach or empty, with plenty or little.

Paul learned to be content, wherever he was, whatever he had. He didn't constantly put himself down as a failure. He wasn't always striving to reach the next level of performance. He was content where he was.

There's a vast chasm between contentment and complacency, and I really think the width of that chasm depends on your heart. If you're honest with yourself, you'll know if you're being complacent. But you'll also know if you're killing yourself to achieve the impossible.

What's the point?
Check your motivation the next time you're stressing out about something. Do you want to be perfect for the glory of God? Or for yourself?

Don't beat yourself up because you can't get there. It doesn't do you any good, and if God would never think horrible things about you because you didn't perform, why is okay for you to think them?

November 4

How to restart in 10 minutes or less

HOW YOU SEE your circumstances determines whether you just get through them or appreciate them.

Hebrews 12:28
Since we are receiving a Kingdom that is unshakable, let us be thankful and please God by worshiping him with holy fear and awe.

There isn't enough gratitude in our world. Very few people really express gratitude as often as they should. I know I don't, and it's a shame because it makes so much difference, not only to the people around you but also to you.

We all have more than we think we do, and taking the time to thank God for everything in our lives forces us to acknowledge it. So take a moment and say thank you. But if you don't mean it, if you aren't really thankful, don't even open your mouth. Thankfulness is a heart thing, and if you're just paying God lip service, it won't help you at all, and it won't impress Him.

What's the point?
Thank Him for the small things. Thank Him for the big things. Thank Him for the good things, and, yes, thank Him for the bad things. Because if you can seriously, honestly thank God for the bad stuff in your life, that bad stuff won't seem so difficult to get through. It won't seem so daunting or frightening or intimidating.

If you want to restart and refresh your perspective, begin with gratitude. It may seem like a small thing, but it changes everything.

November 5

God will provide

IF YOU'RE A Christ follower, you've probably experienced this. You've been sitting in church and listening and all of a sudden you feel an undeniable urge to give money. Or you're walking down the street and you feel this sudden pull to give somebody some money or help somebody out.

Maybe you're a good enough person to just randomly walk around giving people money, but I'm not.

Philippians 4:19
And this same God who takes care of me will supply all your needs from his glorious riches, which have been given to us in Christ Jesus.

Have you ever been in the position to give someone money or a free meal? If you have, you know it's a pretty cool feeling. But in the heat of the moment, when all you can think about is how you live paycheck to paycheck, it's easy to ignore the urge of the Holy Spirit and just do things your own way. But if God has called you to help someone, you need to do it.

You've heard it said that God provides, right? Well, most of the time, God provides through people.

What's the point?
God provides. That's what He does. Sometimes He uses miracles, but most of the time He uses people. But you can trust that if He asks you to do something, He will provide for the hole it leaves.

That's who He is. He is our God who provides what He requires. We just have to trust that He will.

November 6

The lesson my pants taught me

HAVE YOU EVER accidentally given away clothes you still wear on a regular basis? I have. I'm pretty sure that my brand new pair of khaki pants from Old Navy ended up in a donation bag the last time I cleaned my house.

Did I get upset? Well, not really. It's pretty silly to get upset over a pair of khaki pants. But people aren't always rational or logical, and sometimes you just get upset about silly things. In those moments, you can choose to see the situation as a problem or an opportunity.

Philippians 4:11-13
Not that I was ever in need, for I have learned how to be content with whatever I have. I know how to live on almost nothing or with everything. I have learned the secret of living in every situation, whether it is with a full stomach or empty, with plenty or little. For I can do everything through Christ, who gives me strength.

This concept doesn't just apply to khaki pants. Few things in life are irreplaceable, if we're being honest about it. And it's those things that we should focus on. It's those things we should spend our time and effort in obtaining and maintaining.

What's the point?
You have a choice. You can freak out about bad stuff that happens or look for the positive in it.

The less attention you pay to the stuff that isn't going your way, the better you get at focusing on what God is doing in your life.

November 9

The best friends you can have

I HAVE BEEN so very blessed to have such a variety of friends from all corners of the world, all cultures and backgrounds, all personality types. I have friends who are as introverted as I am. I have friends who are insane, crazy people. I have friends who occupy high-ranking corporate positions and friends who work for minimum-wage. And the most beautiful part about all my close friends is that they love Christ, and in the dark moments of my life, they help me remember how much I love Him too.

Proverbs 13:20
Walk with the wise and become wise; associate with fools and get in trouble.

The best friendships I've had are with people who love me for who I am as a person, but they love me too much to let me plateau in my growth—both professionally and spiritually. If you have a friend who just agrees with you all the time that could be nice, but do you ever get to really know that person? The best friends you can have challenge you to grow and love you regardless.

What's the point?
Is there a friend who is open and honest with you in your life? Is there a friend you trust to tell you the truth even if you don't want to hear it? Is there a friend who loves you too much to let you make a foolish decision?

Find that person. Because that person is worth his or her weight in gold. And the more you hang out with wise people like that, the wiser you will become.

November 10

Are the best things in life really free?

THE BEST THINGS in life are free. But are they really?

I mean, I understand what it means. It means that the best parts of life can't be purchased with money. But just because something doesn't cost money doesn't make it free. Everything costs something.

Joshua 24:13-14
I gave you land you had not worked on, and I gave you towns you did not build—the towns where you are now living. I gave you vineyards and olive groves for food, though you did not plant them. "So fear the Lord and serve him wholeheartedly. Put away forever the idols your ancestors worshiped when they lived beyond the Euphrates River and in Egypt."

If we aren't careful, Christians can grow big heads about grace. We live a good life, so we think we deserve it. Maybe we'd never say it out loud, but deep down in our hearts, that's what we think sometimes.

That's what happened to the children of Israel after God delivered them from Egypt. They got used to the luxury of living in the Promised Land, and they forgot to be thankful.

What's the point?
Just be thankful for all that God has given you in your life. All the things you could never replace that God gave you because of His great love.

Don't take them for granted, and never forget that you could never pay the price for them. That's why God had to do it for us.

November 11

Waking up thankful changes your outlook

I'M NOT A morning person—at all. So when I roll out of bed in the morning, I'm grumpy. But every now and then, I wake up, and I feel thankful. Just generally. And it has such an enormous affect on my entire day, it makes me want to wake up that way all the time!

Ephesians 5:20
And give thanks for everything to God the Father in the name of our Lord Jesus Christ.

I focus on my day-to-day goals, on problems I need to overcome. I usually ask God for help, but at the same time, I neglect to thank Him for what He's already done. And that's not how we're supposed to live.

When was the last time I thanked God for my coffee? That sounds silly, but who made coffee? God did. Then, He gave people the brilliant idea to grind it up and boil it in water, and He gave me money to buy it. So God gives me my coffee in the morning. But how often do I remember to thank Him for it?

What's the point?
Be thankful for the big things. Thankful for the small things. Thankful for the good things. And, yes, thankful for the bad things. Thankful for everything.

Wake up. Get your thoughts out of the darkness. Grab your wonderful cup of coffee and take a few moments just to think about what God's already done for you this morning. It just might improve your entire day.

November 12

Saying thanks for what you expect

You don't thank a taxi driver for taking you from point A to point B. You don't thank your barber for cutting your hair. Do you?

I think we jam God and Jesus into this little box. He's the God of Creation. Yes, nice title. He's the Maker of Everything. Also nice title. But what can He do for me?

Luke 17:11-17
As Jesus continued on toward Jerusalem, he reached the border between Galilee and Samaria. As he entered a village there, ten lepers stood at a distance, crying out, "Jesus, Master, have mercy on us!"

He looked at them and said, "Go show yourselves to the priests." And as they went, they were cleansed of their leprosy.

One of them, when he saw that he was healed, came back to Jesus, shouting, "Praise God!" He fell to the ground at Jesus' feet, thanking him for what he had done. This man was a Samaritan.

Jesus asked, "Didn't I heal ten men? Where are the other nine?"

I think we are like the nine sometimes. We recognize that God can help us, but there's a big difference between expecting Him to do great things and believing we deserve it.

What's the point?
Celebrate when God does something great for you. Go tell everybody about it. But before all that, stop. And just say thank you.

God isn't required to do anything for us. He answers our prayers and directs our lives and helps us through difficulty because He wants to.

November 13

Saying thanks versus being thankful

I RECOGNIZE MY good things come from God, but I'm not very good at actually saying thank you as often as I should. I live a busy life. I'm always running around so crazily that I'm never sure if my head is still attached. I'm not sure if I get busy because I can't say no, or if I'm busy because life is busy. But my busyness level should never make me forget to be thankful.

Psalm 103:2
Let all that I am praise the Lord; may I never forget the good things he does for me.

Thanking God for what He's done is like prayer. He already knows that we're thankful, just like He already knows what we're going to pray. It's not for His benefit, it's for ours.

Praying helps us recognize that we can't make it through life on our own. Thanking God for what He's done helps us remember that we didn't accomplish things by ourselves.

What's the point?
On the days when you feel cornered and alone, stop and take the time to write down the things you're thankful for. Make a list of what God has done for you, even if you don't feel like it. They don't have to be huge things. Just ask yourself what God has done for you today.

You will be shocked to realize just how much He's done for you already. I always am.

November 16

Late miracles are still miracles

GOD DOESN'T WORK when we want Him to. He works on His own schedule, and it can be frustrating because His schedule rarely coincides with ours. So while we're waiting for Him to answer our prayers, it's easy to get discouraged, because all you can see is how God opened the doors to allow you to get where you are, and it feels like the next door you need open is stuck.

But the Bible tells us something really important about God that we shouldn't ever forget: God is good.

Isaiah 25:1
O Lord, I will honor and praise your name, for you are my God. You do such wonderful things! You planned them long ago, and now you have accomplished them.

Over and over and over again. God is good. God is good. No one else is good but God. If there's one thing you can know for sure about God, it's the fact that God is good. So when He does work, even if it's not according to what we want, we can still trust that what He's doing is good.

What's the point?
Don't miss the miracles because you're looking at your calendar. God has planned great things in our lives, and He won't stop working until they are all accomplished.

No, He may not accomplish them when we want Him to, but He'll still make it happen because He has promised. So wait, trust, expect, and be thankful for what He's already done.

November 17

Entitlement in blessing

I LOVE TO watch little kids open gifts. They get so excited, and once they have the gift open and know what's inside, they'll usually run around showing everyone. If someone does something nice for you, generally your first reaction is going to be to tell people about it. Isn't it? You'll want to tell your friends and your family and the people you work with that someone you know did something amazing for you.

God is not required to do anything for us. I think we expect God to just do things for us because He's a good God. But we live in such a screwed-up world that the entitlement mentality of our culture has spread to our faith.

1 Chronicles 16:8
Give thanks to the Lord and proclaim his greatness.
Let the whole world know what he has done.

God has done amazing things for us. God is doing amazing things for us, and many times we don't even realize it. So we don't thank Him like we should, and we keep it quiet too.

What's the point?
Think about what God has done for you, because even the "little" things are bigger than we think, too big for us to accomplish on our own.

And once you see the things that God has done for you, tell others about it. Because nothing demonstrates gratitude like telling other people what someone else has done for you.

November 18

Knowing what is good

OUR LIVES ARE full of a lot of things, some good and some not so good. It's funny how we categorize events and people and gifts into good and bad or good and not good. Using our own judgment doesn't always work because we don't know everything. We like to think we do, but we don't. As Christ-followers, we need to depend on Scripture to tell us what is good and what isn't.

Psalm 92:5-7
O Lord, what great works you do!
And how deep are your thoughts.
Only a simpleton would not know,
and only a fool would not understand this:
Though the wicked sprout like weeds
and evildoers flourish,
they will be destroyed forever.

The Bible is full of examples of God teaching us how to think and live. His thoughts are so far beyond our ability to comprehend, and that's why He gave us the Bible—so that we would understand what real goodness actually is.

The world has an idea of what goodness looks like. And they try to get us to accept it as truth, but it contradicts what the Bible says. So as Christ-followers, we should not accept it.

What's the point?
You can be the best person in the world, but you won't innately know what is good or what is bad if the world challenges what you believe. The Bible is the source for what is good, and if you don't know the Bible, you'll be an easy target.

November 19

You can never thank Him enough

DO YOU EVER wake up and just feel the need to be thankful? I get caught up in all the picky little details of life so often. You'd think maybe I'd know better by now, but it seems to be instinctive. It's so easy to get overwhelmed. And then, when I get my head back on straight, I look back and wonder what I was thinking when I was freaking out over nothing.

I fret over things that I can't control anyway, and I marvel at how patient God is with me, especially when I go back and pick up the same worries I promised to lay down.

Psalm 138:1-2
I give you thanks, O Lord,
With all my heart;
I will sing your praises
Before the gods.
I bow before your holy
Temple as I worship.
I praise your name for your
unfailing love and
faithfulness
For your promises are backed
by the honor of your name.

Being thankful is understanding and recognizing that someone has done something for you that they didn't have to do.

What's the point?
If you feel like you need to say thanks to God, do it. If you feel like you don't need to … do it anyway. Because you still need to.

And after a few moments of thanking Him for what He's done, I'm willing to bet that you'll move from needing to thank Him to wanting to thank Him, especially after you really see everything He's done for you.

November 20

Comparing yourself to others wastes time

HAVE YOU EVER sat and watched someone else do your job better than you? Don't say you haven't because we've all been there. We've all watched someone else–someone younger or less experienced or weirder or whatever–do what we do best better than we can do it.

If you're a performance-driven perfectionist like me, it's mortifying. Because nobody should be better than me. If it's my job, I should do it the best in the world.

Galatians 6:4-5
Pay careful attention to your own work, for then you will get the satisfaction of a job well done, and you won't need to compare yourself to anyone else. For we are each responsible for our own conduct.

Nobody can be a better you than you–because you're the only one in existence. God made you exactly the way you are and understood every ridiculous personality quirk before you were even aware of yourself. Something in each of us demands we compare ourselves to the people around us. But you shouldn't.

Comparing yourself to somebody else is a waste of your time, your emotions, and your resources. It gets your focus off what matters–the fact that God put you right where He intended you to be.

What's the point?
Do your best to the glory of God. Period. Don't get caught up in the drama of who did what or why or when. Then, you can look at what you've done and be satisfied.

And, honestly, there's nothing better than being satisfied with a job well done.

November 23

The dangers of arrogance

THIS POST ISN'T really about gratitude, but it is about attitude. I think people struggle sometimes with the difference between being confident and being arrogant.

Habakkuk 2:5
Wealth is treacherous, and the arrogant are never at rest. They open their mouths as wide as the grave, and like death, they are never satisfied. In their greed they have gathered up many nations and swallowed many peoples.

Arrogant people rub everybody the wrong way. So how do you manage when you really just want to pop them in the nose?

What I've learned about arrogant people is that most of the time they brag because they are insecure. So when I run across an arrogant person, I try to look past the bravado and the facade on the outside and see the hurting person underneath. I try to encourage them to be themselves. I try to help the insecurity go away, because if you can eliminate the insecurity, the arrogance fades too.

But there's only so much you can do and you have to be careful.

What's the point?
Give arrogant people a chance. Love them for who they are. Encourage them so that they don't have to feel insecure about whatever it is they feel insecure about. But if they don't listen, if they don't hear, step back.

Get out of their lives. Because arrogant people really are like death: they're never satisfied, they're always greedy, and they won't care who they take down with them.

November 24

The most important part of a letter

TALK TO YOU LATER. Sincerely. Love. Have a great day! Thanks! How do you end letters or emails? How do you decide what to leave people with at the end of a letter or a speech? How you end a letter is just as important as how you start it, and I think that's important concerning the last lines of Bible books too.

The last lines and verses in Scripture aren't always what you would expect. Some are joyful (Matthew). Some are horrifying (Judges). And some seem almost bland, at least until you understand who the letter was written to.

2 Corinthians 13:14
May the grace of the Lord Jesus Christ, the love of God, and the fellowship of the Holy Spirit be with you all.

The Church at Corinth was a mess, and Paul wrote to them addressing the terrible, immoral things they were doing. But he ended his letter with a gentle reminder of where we're supposed to find grace, where we're supposed to seek love and where true fellowship comes from.

How have I ended letters to people I love? Especially in today's text-lingo society. TTYL. LOL. BRB. What good, enriching truth do acronyms for useless expressions communicate? Nothing. Only that I don't want to take the time to spell them out completely.

What's the point?
Don't miss the opportunity to bring hope or encouragement to others. Think about the way you communicate with people, both when you start talking and when you end.

November 25

A gift is a gift

PEOPLE HAVE A hard time accepting gifts. I mean, if it's a special occasion, people will mellow a little. Like Christmas or birthdays, when it's culturally acceptable to give gifts. But generally speaking, if you walk up to someone on the street and try to give them something they could never afford to buy on their own, you'll probably have an argument.

Gratitude is never misplaced when someone gives you a gift. But you don't have to be worthy of a gift. You don't have to earn a gift. If you have to earn it, it becomes a reward.

1 Peter 3:18
Christ suffered for our sins once for all time. He never sinned, but he died for sinners to bring you safely home to God. He suffered physical death, but he was raised to life in the Spirit.

Salvation is an amazing gift. And accepting a gift like that takes humility because to accept it means we are admitting we're not good enough to get to heaven on our own. So we add to God's Word, explaining that we can lose our salvation or that we have to accomplish certain tasks to make it real. And God never said that.

What's the point?
I didn't do anything to earn my salvation. All of my good works amount to nothing in the face of God's pure perfection. And that's not me being overly dramatic or self-deprecating. That's the truth.

When imperfection tries to be perfect, the only result will be frustration. That's why God doesn't ask us to be perfect. He asks us to believe.

November 26
The lost holiday

THANKSGIVING GETS lost in American culture. Nestled between Halloween and Christmas, the stores rarely put out Thanksgiving decorations anymore. They just have sales on food. It isn't that people don't celebrate it. I think it's just that Americans are so fat and happy all the time that a day devoted solely to eating and watching football isn't that unusual anymore.

I think Americans have forgotten what it is that we're celebrating.

Psalm 100:4-5
Enter his gates with thanksgiving;
go into his courts with praise.
Give thanks to him and praise his name.
For the Lord is good.
His unfailing love continues forever,
and his faithfulness continues to each generation.

Americans can be thankful for so many reasons. We are one of the wealthiest countries on Earth, and God has blessed us in every way possible. But blessings don't just happen. America is blessed because the people who founded it followed God. America is still blessed because there are many others who still follow God.

God has been faithful to us for all these centuries. Every generation has experienced His love, but all it takes for the next generation to forget is for the current generation to stay silent.

What's the point?
We have so much to be thankful for. And while Halloween is fun and Christmas is epic, we shouldn't forget the little holiday in between. Because if we forget to be thankful, we'll lose more than just a holiday.

November 27

A gift worth more than it costs

CHRISTMAS IS ONE of those holidays that everybody can celebrate, regardless of wealth or status. To me, the best kind of gifts represent something. They may not be the most expensive gifts on the shelf, but they mean something deeper than a price tag can communicate.

Mark 12:41-44
Jesus sat down near the collection box in the Temple and watched as the crowds dropped in their money. Many rich people put in large amounts. Then a poor widow came and dropped in two small coins. Jesus called his disciples to him and said, "I tell you the truth, this poor widow has given more than all the others who are making contributions. For they gave a tiny part of their surplus, but she, poor as she is, has given everything she had to live on."

This is one of my favorite stories from the life of Christ. Not everyone would notice a lowly widow dropping worthless coins into an offering box. Such an action would be lost amid the hustle and bustle of the big givers. But it wasn't about cost with her; it was about worth. And she believed that giving her all to God was worth it.

What's the point?
When it comes to giving gifts, we need to learn to look beyond the price tag.

Just because something costs a lot doesn't mean it's worth a lot, and, likewise, a gift that seems to cost very little might be worth more than the wealthiest man can pay.

November 30

The best gift you ever received

WHAT'S THE BEST Christmas present you've ever received? Do you remember it? A friend asked me that this weekend, and the answer popped into my head almost immediately. It would have been Christmas of 1992 or 1993, and I remember coming down the stairs to see a beautiful wooden dollhouse, made by my grandparents.

But sometimes the best gifts aren't under the tree. Even that dollhouse—what made it so special to me was that my grandparents took the time and effort to make something so beautiful for me.

2 Corinthians 4:18
So we don't look at the troubles we can see now; rather, we fix our gaze on things that cannot be seen. For the things we see now will soon be gone, but the things we cannot see will last forever.

Christmas is almost here. People will be gathering together soon. I know the stress of the holidays can be overwhelming, but let me encourage you to take a moment to be thankful for a great gift in your life—the people who love you.

Think what your life would look like without them. Think who you would be without them. Nothing wrapped up in a bow with pretty paper could ever mean more to me than a moment with any of them.

What's the point?
Outside of our salvation through Christ, there's no greater gift in our lives than time with the people we love.

Make the most of it this Christmas. Don't miss the opportunity to enjoy the gift of your loved ones this year.

December 2015

HOW TO BE HAPPY

We have more than any other culture in history—more money, more food, more possessions, more everything. But somehow we are the most unhappy people in the world. So if you can't find happiness when you have everything you want, can you find happiness at all?

The Bible says yes. But what God says will bring us happiness usually always goes against what the world tells us.

December 1
How to be happy

HAPPINESS DERIVED from circumstances can change, so if you are happy because your circumstances are happy, it won't last. But happiness derived from knowing Christ is solid and strong and unchanging. Even if your circumstances change, God doesn't. And that's why, as believers, we can be happy even if our situation isn't.

Philippians 1:9-11
I pray that your love will overflow more and more, and that you will keep on growing in knowledge and understanding. For I want you to understand what really matters, so that you may live pure and blameless lives until the day of Christ's return. May you always be filled with the fruit of your salvation—the righteous character produced in your life by Jesus Christ—for this will bring much glory and praise to God.

I'm going to work today, but my job isn't what really matters. What matters is the people there. It's just a job, but the way I live can allow me to be Jesus to the people around me. And that does matter. Because when the day is over, the job will still be there; but the people around me might not be.

If we take that perspective with everything in our lives, I think our attitudes might change.

What's the point?
Understand what's important to God and make that a priority in your life. Stop spending so much time and energy on the details that don't matter. Stop fretting over pieces of your life that won't make a difference in eternity.

Identify what really matters and what really doesn't. And let the other stuff go.

December 2

Stuff happens for a reason

LIFE HAS NEVER been easy. Life is life, so it's screwed up because people are screwed up, but I've found I can make it through just about anything as long as there's a purpose for it.

There's a purpose to everything. God isn't a god of chaos, and nothing surprises Him. So when stuff happens in our lives, it doesn't shake Him, and it doesn't make Him worry. It's all part of His plan, and He can use it to accomplish something amazing.

Philippians 1:12-14
And I want you to know, my dear brothers and sisters, that everything that has happened to me here has helped to spread the Good News. For everyone here, including the whole palace guard, knows that I am in chains because of Christ. And because of my imprisonment, most of the believers here have gained confidence and boldly speak God's message without fear.

Stuff happens in our lives, and most of the time there's nothing we can do about it. It's all we can do to keep our heads above water, and after the storms keep coming without any relief, we can get discouraged. We can become unhappy. But we need to remember that no matter what happens, there's a reason.

What's the point?
Whatever you're facing today, whether it's circumstances you don't deserve or circumstances your actions have caused, remember that stuff happens for a reason. And if God's in it, that's reason enough to rejoice because He can use it. So you have a reason to be happy.

December 3

God can use impure motives

IT'S EASY FOR me to stress out about the condition of the world. And I've had such a negative experience with so many churches, it's easy for me to get pretty unhappy and angry at Christians too.

Philippians 1:15-19
It's true that some are preaching out of jealousy and rivalry. But others preach about Christ with pure motives. They preach because they love me, for they know I have been appointed to defend the Good News. Those others do not have pure motives as they preach about Christ. They preach with selfish ambition, not sincerely, intending to make my chains more painful to me. But that doesn't matter. Whether their motives are false or genuine, the message about Christ is being preached either way, so I rejoice. And I will continue to rejoice. For I know that as you pray for me and the Spirit of Jesus Christ helps me, this will lead to my deliverance.

Just as we have "preachers" and "ministers" who really only work for selfish reasons, Paul seems to have encountered the same folks in the first century. But Paul doesn't care why they're telling others about Christ. He's just happy that they're doing it.

What's the point?
If someone is doing the right thing but you suspect they're doing it for the wrong reasons–don't worry about it.

Focusing on someone else's motivation will only distract you from your purpose. Let God sort out the hearts of others. He's big enough to use anyone—even people with impure motives.

December 4

Even pirates have a code

A RELATIONSHIP with Christ is freedom, that's true. But part of being a Christian is living like one, and while there are no requirements for worthiness, there is a code of conduct that a Christ-follower should submit to. Part of that is loving each other and finding common ground.

Philippians 1:27
Above all, you must live as citizens of heaven, conducting yourselves in a manner worthy of the Good News about Christ. Then, whether I come and see you again or only hear about you, I will know that you are standing together with one spirit and one purpose, fighting together for the faith, which is the Good News.

Citizens of heaven are the Christ-followers. So if you believe in Jesus, you are a citizen of Heaven, and you are supposed to act like it, which means we're supposed to get along with other believers. Even if the only common ground you can find is that you both believe that Christ died for your sins, stand there. That's the most important point, and if you agree on that, everything else is insignificant. Or at least, it should be.

What's the point?
Maybe you're surrounded by Christians you don't like or who don't agree with you, but that doesn't give you a reason to fight with them.

Who knows? That old-fashioned religious person you just can't stop fighting with might end up in the mansion next door to you through all of eternity. So you'd better figure out how to get along.

December 7

Seeing suffering as a privilege

OUR WORLD THRIVES on intimidation because the whole world is insecure, and insecure people feel like they must criticize people around them so they feel better about their failures. The world hates Christ-followers because it hates itself; it just won't admit it. So of course the world is going to try to tear us apart.

When that happens, we can either crumble, or we can hold our ground and love them like Christ did. But be warned, if people can't intimidate you, they'll try to hurt you. And while you can't control the people who want to hurt you, you can control how you respond to the hurt.

Philippians 1:28-30
Don't be intimidated in any way by your enemies. This will be a sign to them that they are going to be destroyed, but that you are going to be saved, even by God himself. For you have been given not only the privilege of trusting in Christ but also the privilege of suffering for him. We are in this struggle together. You have seen my struggle in the past, and you know that I am still in the midst of it.

As Christ-followers, we're never supposed to repay hurt with hurt. We need to love every person who hates us. So when you suffer for your faith, don't see it as a problem. See it as an opportunity to get closer to God.

What's the point?
When you're facing a bully, don't cower and give in to their demands. Don't lash out with hateful words or actions. Take the abuse and love them back. Love them in spite of themselves.

The moment you fold and lower yourself to their level, they win. And you will have lost your chance to show them how strong God really is.

December 8

Contentment never comes by comparison

I THINK ONE reason people can't get along is because we only focus on how different we are from each other. We only see our differences, so we assume we have nothing in common. Then we form opinions or give in to preconceived notions, and before we know it, we convince ourselves that we'll never get along.

Philippians 2:1-2
Is there any encouragement from belonging to Christ? Any comfort from his love? Any fellowship together in the Spirit? Are your hearts tender and compassionate? Then make me truly happy by agreeing wholeheartedly with each other, loving one another, and working together with one mind and purpose.

We aren't supposed to be the same people. God made us different and put us in different circumstances with different life experiences so that where one person is weak the other person can be strong. But because we like to compare ourselves, because we refuse to be happy with where we are, we only see the differences. So we don't see how our differences can make us strong through Christ.

What's the point?
Stop comparing yourself to other people. Stop looking at other people's lives and wondering why they deserve to be happy when you don't. Reach out to someone you don't know. Prove your preconceived notions wrong. I guarantee you will.

And even if the person you reach out to turns out to be exactly opposite from you, you still have one thing in common. And that one thing, Christ, can make up for everything else.

December 9

Comparison and focus are different

BY THE WORLD'S thinking, it doesn't make sense to sacrifice what you could spend on yourself to spend on someone else. But as believers we aren't called to live by the world's philosophy, and let's just be honest, what has the world's thinking accomplished?

There's a big difference between comparing ourselves to others around us and focusing on them.

Philippians 2:3-4
Don't be selfish; don't try to impress others. Be humble, thinking of others as better than yourselves. Don't look out only for your own interests, but take an interest in others, too.

You would think that focusing only on yourself and trying to make yourself happy would work. You would think that if you spent all your time and all your money on making yourself happy you would be. You'd think that if you spent all your energy in an attempt to bring yourself contentment that you would accomplish it. But the more you live for yourself, the more unhappy you will be.

What's the point?
You can focus on other people without comparing yourself to them. You can live for other people. You can care about what they care about. You can make sure that other people have what they need to succeed.

Want to be happy? Focus on others. And the more you give to other people, the happier you will be.

December 10

Choose your attitude

I WAS HIRED to be a webmaster and a writer, but my first few weeks on the job, I spent the majority of my time as a pack horse. My manager at the time kept apologizing because hauling boxes and heavy equipment wasn't why I was hired. But I had already chosen to be cheerful. I needed the exercise anyway.

Philippians 2:5-8
You must have the same attitude that Christ Jesus had. Though he was God, he did not think of equality with God as something to cling to. Instead, he gave up his divine privileges; he took the humble position of a slave and was born as a human being. When he appeared in human form, he humbled himself in obedience to God and died a criminal's death on a cross.

Attitude is everything. If your attitude is sour, your perspective will be sour. It colors everything. But you can choose your attitude. You decide when you roll out of bed what your attitude is going to be today.

No, you can't control the events of the day. No, you can't control your circumstances. No, you can't control other people. But you can control how you react. You can control how you respond. You can control what you think. And while you may not be able to control how you feel, you can choose how you act on your feelings.

What's the point?
You can't choose your circumstances. But you can choose how you face them. Jesus chose His attitude. Choose yours.

December 11

Happiness in spite of a broken heart

SOMETHING ABOUT recognizing that you are broken allows God to truly do what He wants to do in your life. I don't know if it's because you aren't hiding. I don't know if it's because you're being honest with God and with yourself and with everyone else. I don't know. But the humility that comes from understanding how broken we are is something that God can take and make beautiful.

Philippians 2:9-11
Therefore, God elevated him to the place of highest honor and gave him the name above all other names,
that at the name of Jesus every knee should bow,
in heaven and on earth and under the earth,
and every tongue confess that Jesus Christ is Lord,
to the glory of God the Father.

My life really hasn't worked out the way I thought it would. Instead, God has allowed me to do things I never thought I'd get to do. He has opened doors for me to help others in ways I never could have if I had been married and had children, like I had planned. But before He could use me the way He wanted, I had to let go of the dreams I had for me.

What's the point?

Wherever you are today, God can take a broken heart and make it beautiful again. But you've got to be willing to let go of what you think you deserve.

If you can do that, you'll be surprised where you end up, and you'll be amazed what He gives you the opportunity to do.

December 14

Get off the couch

IT'S EASY TO work when someone is supervising you. When your boss is around, it's easy to do what they want. When your parents are around, it's easy to do the things that make them happy. And in making them happy, you feel happy. But when you're on your own, it's not so easy. You have to be self-motivated, and self-motivation is difficult.

Philippians 2:12-13
Dear friends, you always followed my instructions when I was with you. And now that I am away, it is even more important. Work hard to show the results of your salvation, obeying God with deep reverence and fear. For God is working in you, giving you the desire and the power to do what pleases him.

If you know Christ, and if you've chosen to follow Him, He will give you not only the desire to do His will but also the power to make it happen.

Can you still choose to sit on the couch and veg? Sure. But will you be happy? Maybe you'll think you are for a little while, but you won't really be. If you're a Christ-follower, you have a purpose here. God has something for you to do, and if you're ignoring it, you're going to be discontent. It's like a Sheltie stuck indoors with nowhere to run. You're wired to do something specific, and if you refuse to do it, you'll be restless and unhappy until you do.

What's the point?
Want to be happy, American Christian?

Get off the couch and get to work.

December 15

Complaining is normal but not helpful

COMPLAINING USUALLY makes us feel better, but it doesn't accomplish anything. It doesn't actually satisfy either. Maybe it makes you feel better for a little while, but it doesn't last because nothing changes. It just drags you deeper into depression, and usually you end up taking other people with you.

Philippians 2:14-15
Do everything without complaining and arguing, so that no one can criticize you. Live clean, innocent lives as children of God, shining like bright lights in a world full of crooked and perverse people.

Ouch. Notice it doesn't say live for Christ without complaining. It doesn't say work without complaining. It doesn't say serve without complaining. It says everything. Whatever you do, wherever you go, whatever you're dealing with, do it without either complaining or arguing. Double ouch.

It's normal to complain. It's normal to blame God for your problems. It's normal to argue with people. But as Christ-followers, we aren't called to be normal. We are called to be different. We're supposed to stand out. We're supposed to be obvious, shining like stars against the black backdrop of the empty void of space.

What's the point?
Stop blaming God. Stop arguing with other people. Focus on what you're called to do and be thankful that God has a use for you. And while you wait for further instruction, praise God for who He is and what He's done.

I guarantee you won't be able to complain when you're thanking God for what you have.

December 16
Little is much

DO YOU WANT to do something amazing for God? Maybe you don't. Maybe you're more comfortable sitting on the sidelines and never jumping into a ministry, and that's okay if you're satisfied with a life that doesn't make a real difference. But if you're the kind of Christ-follower who wants God to be pleased, what do you do with yourself?

Philippians 2:16-18
Hold firmly to the word of life; then, on the day of Christ's return, I will be proud that I did not run the race in vain and that my work was not useless. But I will rejoice even if I lose my life, pouring it out like a liquid offering to God, just like your faithful service is an offering to God. And I want all of you to share that joy. Yes, you should rejoice, and I will share your joy.

I get frustrated because I can't do more for God. I try to squeeze things into my calendar until I'm so overwhelmed with busyness I don't even know which end is up anymore. What stands out to me in this verse is a pretty simple concept: Faithful service is an offering to God.

Are you doing something to serve other people right now? Do you look at it as something that doesn't matter? Something that's not important? That's a lie. If you are helping someone else, you're a hero.

What's the point?
Be faithful in your service to others in the name of Christ, and you will make a difference for God.

Even if it's small, God has a habit of taking small things and making them huge.

December 17

Whatever happens

SOMETIMES LIFE JUST happens, and it's all you can do to drag yourself out of bed. You know you're going to face another day working at a job that stresses you out, or you're going to face an unpleasant situation you can't control. And all you want to do in those moments is sit down and cry.

So why is it important to keep looking up when those moments come?

Philippians 3:1
Whatever happens, my dear brothers and sisters, rejoice in the Lord. I never get tired of telling you these things, and I do it to safeguard your faith.

Choosing to have joy is a hard thing, especially when you're struggling emotionally. Choosing to be thankful even for the bad things in life is challenging because it's so much easier to give up.

But if you give up, you're stepping out of a story that's bigger than you. If you give up, you're choosing to believe that God can't use a difficult situation. You're choosing to believe that God is unable or unwilling, and that's not true.

What's the point?

God has good plans for us, but God rarely snaps His fingers to make them happen. Usually we need to grow up a little too. But if we can hold on through the dark days, our faith will get stronger because God will prove Himself over and over.

Later on down the road, He'll usually give us what we asked for. But first, we have to want Him more than our own dreams.

December 18

Good enough

THE LAW IS good. God gave us the law to establish order and peace, and–well–many of the Ten Commandments are moral laws too. But the law becomes dangerous when you convince yourself that you can be good enough. And for a little while, you'll be okay. Because if you're a good enough person, you can be a good enough Christian in comparison to others, but what happens when you screw up?

Philippians 3:2-4
Watch out for those dogs, those people who do evil, those mutilators who say you must be circumcised to be saved. For we who worship by the Spirit of God are the ones who are truly circumcised. We rely on what Christ Jesus has done for us. We put no confidence in human effort, though I could have confidence in my own effort if anyone could. Indeed, if others have reason for confidence in their own efforts, I have even more!

A portion of the Bible is devoted to teaching us how to live, but trouble comes when you take the lifestyle that the Bible promotes and turn it into something that redeems us. No lifestyle will redeem you. No dress code will make you perfect. All following the Law does is show us that we aren't good enough.

What's the point?
Obey the law, but don't trust your eternity to it. Wearing the burden of perfection is exhausting. You can't be perfect, and trying to be just wears you out.

Trying to be perfect doesn't bring happiness; it just brings weariness.

December 21

Truly valuable

MANY TIMES WE value things that don't matter, and as a result we are often unhappy. What you value is what you will seek, and if you value something that doesn't satisfy, you'll be unhappy.

Philippians 3:7-11
I once thought these things were valuable, but now I consider them worthless because of what Christ has done. Yes, everything else is worthless when compared with the infinite value of knowing Christ Jesus my Lord. For his sake I have discarded everything else, counting it all as garbage, so that I could gain Christ and become one with him. I no longer count on my own righteousness through obeying the law; rather, I become righteous through faith in Christ. For God's way of making us right with himself depends on faith. I want to know Christ and experience the mighty power that raised him from the dead. I want to suffer with him, sharing in his death, so that one way or another I will experience the resurrection from the dead!

So many times, we value what the world says is important. Or we value what religion tells us is important. But do those things truly matter? What makes us right with God is faith in Jesus. It's nothing we do. It's nothing we wear. It's nothing we achieve. Just believing that Christ paid the price for us. And though it's not easy, it is simple. And whether we will admit it or not, there is joy in simple things.

What's the point?
Don't let the heaviness of your own righteousness convince you that it's worth something. It's not.

December 22

Get your head out of yesterday

I'VE NEVER SEEN a runner trying to compete by running forward and looking backward. I'm sure people do it because people are strange, but I'd be willing to bet, they don't run well. Because even if you find a way to look backward as you're running forward, your focus won't be where it needs to be–on the goal.

Philippians 3:12-14
I don't mean to say that I have already achieved these things or that I have already reached perfection. But I press on to possess that perfection for which Christ Jesus first possessed me. No, dear brothers and sisters, I have not achieved it, but I focus on this one thing: Forgetting the past and looking forward to what lies ahead, I press on to reach the end of the race and receive the heavenly prize for which God, through Christ Jesus, is calling us.

The past is important. We need to remember where we've been and recognize what God wants us to learn from where we've been. But you can't focus on yesterday. What's done is done and can't be changed; what can change is how you deal with it.

What's the point?
You can learn from yesterday. Just don't live there.

Keep your eyes forward. Don't worry about the other runners; they'll handle themselves. Don't worry about the road behind you; it's past. Don't worry about the road ahead of you; take it a day at a time.

December 23

Agree or disagree but keep moving

MAJOR DISAGREEMENTS happen in the church all the time. Even if you have an awesome church, disagreements are still going to happen. Why? Because everybody is different. We all look at each other differently. We all look at life differently. Our different experiences in life have shaped the way we live. And these differences extend to our walk with God too.

Philippians 3:15-16
Let all who are spiritually mature agree on these things. If you disagree on some point, I believe God will make it plain to you. But we must hold on to the progress we have already made.

There are a lot of Christians in the world. Christians are people who believe Jesus paid the price for their sins and, because of Him alone, they are going to heaven and they can have a relationship with God. They're everywhere, in every country. But if you put them all in the same room, it's very likely that none of them will agree on anything else.

Cultures are different. Personalities are different. Everything is different.

But no matter if your disagreement is with someone who doesn't believe or with someone who does, the way to deal with it is the same: Agree on what matters. Let God work everything else out. And keep moving forward.

What's the point?
You won't agree with everyone. And not everyone will agree with you. Get over it. You can focus on the perspectives that you share. And even if nobody agrees, you can still be civil.

December 24

Something to remember

WITH THE PRESSURES of daily life, especially during the holiday season, it's so easy to forget that God is going to come back for us. It's so easy to get buried in this life and think this is all there is. But this isn't all there is. This world isn't home.

Philippians 4:4-5
Always be full of joy in the Lord. I say it again—rejoice! Let everyone see that you are considerate in all you do. Remember, the Lord is coming soon.

Remember, the Lord is coming soon.

I've always seen that as a warning, but what if it isn't? Remember, the Lord is coming soon, so when you don't feel like rejoicing, you still have something to rejoice about. Remember, the Lord is coming soon, so when you're so bogged down with your own troubles that you can't invest in others, you still have something to look forward to.

God is preparing a place for us that defies explanation, and we will get to live there with Him for all eternity. That is our home. Not this broken, worn down shell of a world we turned over to Satan thousands of years ago.

What's the point?
When everything goes wrong, rejoice. When everything goes right, rejoice. Choose to have an attitude that makes you unsinkable.

But above all else, remember, the Lord is coming soon. The world won't go on like this forever, and when the ticking clock of Time finally winds down, all of us who know Christ will get to go on living with Him.

December 25
The world is not enough

I GET TIRED of the world. I get tired of living in such a broken place, where what used to be good is now called bad and what used to be bad is now called good. I hate to see people hurting, and I get so tired of having to overcome obstacles in my own life when I don't feel like I've really done anything to deserve them.

You live the way you're supposed to. You keep the faith. You treat others the way you want to be treated. You love God. You love people. And everything still goes wrong. What point could there possibly be to living like that?

Philippians 3:20-21
But we are citizens of heaven, where the Lord Jesus Christ lives. And we are eagerly waiting for him to return as our Savior. He will take our weak mortal bodies and change them into glorious bodies like his own, using the same power with which he will bring everything under his control.

We aren't supposed to have a comfortable, easy life on Earth because Earth isn't our final destination. We aren't supposed to hoard all our money and resources so we can sit back in our easy chairs with our remote controls and our cups of coffee and watch television all day long. We were designed for more than that.

What's the point?
Life will be difficult, but God is good.

The more uncomfortable we are, the easier it is to remember that this world isn't our home.

December 28

Worry steals your peace

WORRY IS AN insidious sin, stealthy and nagging. Even when you think you've mastered it, worry will continue to creep up behind you and whisper in your ear. But worry can be forced away.

Worrying is a choice. It's just like anything else we choose to think about. We don't have to let our minds do whatever they want.

Philippians 4:6-7
Don't worry about anything; instead, pray about everything. Tell God what you need, and thank him for all he has done. Then you will experience God's peace, which exceeds anything we can understand. His peace will guard your hearts and minds as you live in Christ Jesus.

Worry drags us down. It turns us into people who aren't much fun to be around. And it's absolutely the easiest sin to fall into because it seems harmless. I mean, how is my worrying going to hurt someone else? Well, it doesn't start off hurting others. It starts off by hurting you. If all your energy is focused on worrying, you will begin to see the damage physically, emotionally, and spiritually. Soon after, it will raise a barrier between you and people who love you.

What's the point?
As long as you hold on to worry and anxiety, you won't know peace. And if you don't know peace, you're not going to be happy.

Whatever you're worrying about, put it down. Stop focusing on it. Change your mind about it and focus on what God is doing instead.

December 29

We become what we think about

SOME PEOPLE operate under the assumption that we can't choose what we think about. But that's not true. Just because your brain starts thinking about something, that doesn't mean you have to think about it.

Philippians 4:8-9
And now, dear brothers and sisters, one final thing. Fix your thoughts on what is true, and honorable, and right, and pure, and lovely, and admirable. Think about things that are excellent and worthy of praise. Keep putting into practice all you learned and received from me—everything you heard from me and saw me doing. Then the God of peace will be with you.

What I think about affects my attitude and my perspective. If I think about the things I don't have that I still want, I become discontent and unhappy. If my brain wanders down the road of any random topic with a negative bent, it won't be long before the rest of me follows right along. What I spend my time thinking about shapes my mood and my attitude and my conversation and my choices.

What's the point?
We can choose what we think about, and we need to choose to think things that are true and right and good. Each thought we have is a seed, and we need to choose which ones are worthy of nurturing and which ones need to be thrown away.

We become what we think about. So it's a good idea to think about something worth the time.

December 30

Some choices are better than others

SOMETIMES I GET discouraged with where God has me. I want to do more and bigger things for God, and that's not wrong.

Many people have been killed for their faith in Christ, and God always uses that. But you don't have to die for your faith for God to use you.

Philippians 1:20-26
For I fully expect and hope that I will never be ashamed, but that I will continue to be bold for Christ, as I have been in the past. And I trust that my life will bring honor to Christ, whether I live or die. For to me, living means living for Christ, and dying is even better. But if I live, I can do more fruitful work for Christ. So I really don't know which is better. I'm torn between two desires: I long to go and be with Christ, which would be far better for me. But for your sakes, it is better that I continue to live. Knowing this, I am convinced that I will remain alive so I can continue to help all of you grow and experience the joy of your faith. And when I come to you again, you will have even more reason to take pride in Christ Jesus because of what he is doing through me.

What's the point?
You want to make a difference for Christ? Yeah. Dying for your faith is a good choice.

But you can be Jesus to your brothers and sisters in Christ, and that can make just as much difference.

December 31
The secret to happiness

WHAT IS THE secret to being happy? Is there a magic formula? Can you just mix up some random things and expect to create happiness for yourself? Is it at the end of a rainbow, like a pot of gold?

Life can be so dark sometimes. People have to endure so many things, so many hurts, so many disappointments. Is there a secret to happiness?

Philippians 4:13
For I can do everything through Christ, who gives me strength.

If there's a secret to being content, to being happy with life, it's right here. No matter what you're going through, no matter where you are, no matter what you have or what you don't have, you have strength to do everything because Christ is with you. Christ gives us strength for the bad days. Christ gives us strength for the good days. So whether you're celebrating a win or mourning a loss, you can still be happy because you can trust that Christ will strengthen you no matter what.

What's the point?
I don't have to be afraid of the future, because with Christ I can handle whatever is coming.

I don't have to regret the past, because with Christ I can learn from my mistakes and leave them behind me.

I can love people, I can rejoice in difficulty, I can live without worry, and I can be secure enough to disagree with people I respect because Christ gives me the strength.

If that doesn't make you happy, nothing will.

Bible Verse Index

Old Testament

New Testament